REA ACI Y0-ABQ-985

Devotions for Debtors

Devotions for Debtors

Kristen Johnson Ingram

GALILEE/DOUBLEDAY

NEW YORK LONDON
TORONTO SYDNEY AUCKLAND

A GALILEE BOOK
PUBLISHED BY DOUBLEDAY
a division of Random House, Inc.

GALILEE and DOUBLEDAY are registered trademarks of Random
House, Inc., and the portrayal of a ship with a cross above a
book is a trademark of Random House, Inc.

First Galilee edition published February 2004

Book design by Ellen Cipriano

Devotions for Debtors was originally published by Crossings Book
Club in 2002.

Library of Congress Cataloging-in-Publication Data
Ingram, Kristen Johnson.
Devotions for debtors / Kristen Johnson Ingram.—1st Galilee ed.
   p.   cm.
1. Debt—Prayer-books and devotions—English.
2. Finance, Personal—Prayer books
and devotions—English.   I. Title

BV4647.T5154 2004
242'.68—dc21   2003053911

ISBN 0-385-51078-0

PRINTED IN THE UNITED STATES OF AMERICA

10 9 8 7 6 5 4 3 2 1

Especially for Linda Clare,
with my gratitude

Devotions for Debtors

Traveling Light

[Jesus] ordered them to take nothing for their
journey except a staff; no bread, no bag, no money in
their belts; but to wear sandals and not to put on
two tunics.

—Mark 6:8, 9

I wonder how much faster turtles could travel if
they didn't have to carry their houses with them.
Without that heavy shell, turtles could slither over
the rocks as fast as their cousins, the lizards. If birds
had to carry such a load, they'd never get off the
ground!

Possessions and the debt I incurred for them are
slowing me down. I have too many things that need
taking care of: clothes to wash and fold and put
away, plants to water and feed, knickknacks and fur-
niture to dust and sometimes repair, so much food
I don't know what's in the freezer. And worrying
about paying for all those things is heavier than any
turtle shell in the world.

I'm going to start traveling lighter. I can get along with a lot less than I have, and being debt-free will let me move through life without a burden.

ℬ For Further Reflection

Write down ten things you don't need or even want very much. Decide what you'll do with them: give them to charity, pass them on to a family member, or sell them at a garage sale. Every time you get rid of something, reward yourself by listening to music, calling a friend, or having a cup of hot chocolate.

ℬ Prayer

Dear Lord, turn me from turtle to bird. Help me to unload my burdens today. Amen

A Mind That Can Learn

Why should fools have a price in hand to buy
wisdom, when they have no mind to learn?
                                    —Proverbs 17:16

Some people *can't* learn because they have a physical problem that prevents their brains from accepting and retaining data.

But others—and sometimes I'm one of them—*won't* learn. Although I have normal intelligence, I ignore the lessons of debt. When I receive a big payment or a windfall, I pay off all my credit cards—and in no time, I start running them up again.

When the Bible calls someone "fool," it means someone who is too stubborn to look at the truth of anything. I don't want to be stubborn, so now I'm trying to think over the lessons of debt. Debt, of course, means paying interest, which robs me of cash I need for everyday living. But what's worse is, debt robs me of peace.

I'd be a *real* fool to think God ever intended me to lie awake at night with a knot in my stomach.

For Further Reflection

Nobody likes to admit to being foolish. But debtors have failed to learn how to live without credit. Decide *today* that you're going to listen to your own good sense, and quit running up those bills. Mark this day on your calendar.

Prayer

Eternal God, you have given me a mind that can learn. Now, teach me how to use it. Amen

Forgiving Debts

And forgive us our debts, as we also have forgiven our debtors.

—Matthew 6:12

I haven't just *incurred* debts. People owe *me*.

I've done favors for friends who never did any for me. Sometimes I took care of their unruly kids for longer than I expected. Or I paid for *every* lunch we had together. Maybe I let them borrow books they never returned, or transported them each week to the doctor in another city without being compensated for gas.

Many of those people are no longer in my life. I've lost touch with some of them, or they've moved away. One of these people actually turned on me and hurt me.

Perhaps the reason I have been unable to stay out of debt is that deep down, I haven't *really* forgiven all those debts. Even though the Lord's Prayer says "forgive me as I forgive," I've been unconsciously keeping score in my heart. So now I'm going to consciously dismiss anything that anyone owes me. The tally between us is going to be clear from now on.

For Further Reflection

1. On a sheet of paper, write the words "your debt is forgiven."
2. Beneath those words, list the names of people who never repaid favor or money, or who never returned your belongings.
3. Ask God to help you forgive and *forget* all those unpaid items.
4. Burn the sheet of paper to show you've released those people from your debt.

Prayer

God, you forgive my sins and forget them. Give me a mind like yours. Amen

Satisfaction

The lover of money will not be satisfied with money;
nor the lover of wealth, with gain.

—*Ecclesiastes 5:10*

I used to take my pleasure in small things. A cup of fresh tea in my grandmother's china cup, a walk in the snowy woods to look for the first violets, rereading a book of poetry, visiting with a friend—all these were where I found my joy. I was centered.

But somewhere, I jumped on the worldly bandwagon, and began *wanting*. A bigger house, a newer car, a cell phone, a quieter printer, more expensive clothes. I had to have faster computers with unbelievable memories.

A wanting heart is never filled. No matter what I have, I'll always want more, unless I travel back to my own center where God alone can satisfy my restless longings. Today, instead of shopping, I'm going for a walk. Afterwards, I'll take down my grandmother's blue and white teacup and brew a fresh pot of black tea. And I'm going to give thanks.

For Further Reflection

Make a list of ten free things or activities you enjoy. Then actually engage in two or three of them, and pray words of thanksgiving so that you can take your joy in simplicity.

Prayer

King of heaven, once you taught me to find joy within myself. Help me find it again. Amen

Longing for Power

Men cry out under a load of oppression; they plead
for relief from the arm of the powerful. But no one
says, "Where is God my Maker, who gives songs in
the night, who teaches more to us than to the beasts
of the earth and makes us wiser than the birds of
the air?"

—Job 35:9–11

Credit card companies often tell us we can have "purchasing *power*." Cool—but isn't the desire for power the most ancient of sins? After all, the serpent in Eden invited Eve to eat forbidden fruit to know all things, saying, "You will be like God."

I think I feel powerful when I slap my credit card down in a restaurant, or order books from online stores, or buy expensive gifts for friends. But I suspect that the urge for power—besides sending me into debt—could eventually turn me into someone I don't like, instead of making me more like the Almighty.

The gifts of God are a million times stronger than "purchasing power." If I ask for grace or forgiveness or guidance, I receive them without having to pay. God has bestowed on me an appreciation for nature, and the joy of family. And these gifts are a lot easier to appropriate because God doesn't have a credit limit. Or impose a carrying charge.

For Further Reflection

1. Do you feel powerless in some area of your life?
2. Are you trying to overcome that powerlessness by buying things or showing off?
3. What does God offer you instead?

Prayer

The kingdom, the power, and the glory are yours, Father in Heaven. Amen

Thou Shalt Not Sneak

Would not God discover this? For he knows the secrets of the heart.

—Psalm 44:21

I never thought I'd do such a thing. I got to the mailbox before my husband did, and I hid the department store bill. I rationalized that in a week I'd have the money to pay the bill, and I could give him bill and payment at the same time.

Which I did. The bill is wiped out, but my conscience is still stinging, and I asked myself whether sneaking is a by-product of debt, or is debt the outcome of a dishonest attitude?

My parents were closemouthed about money, and my mother let me think we were rather poor. When her illness and old age meant I had to take over her finances, I was surprised at her sizable bank accounts (which we had to spend for her care). I didn't inherit her money, but I got a good-sized share of her financial denial—in reverse. She hid her money; I hide my debt.

And sneaking has to be the worst thing in the world. I'm not going to keep living lies.

✍ For Further Reflection

Fold a piece of paper in half. On one side, write the small ways in which you're dishonest, sneaky, or in denial about money. On the other half, write what you'll do to remedy that pattern of behavior.

✍ Prayer

Dear Lord, you said the truth would set me free. Help me free myself. Amen

Lobster Claws

Have you journeyed to the springs of the sea or
walked in the recesses of the deep?

—Job 38:16

The glass aquarium in our market holds several lobsters that move lethargically through the water.
They would probably do battle over the small terri-
tory, but their claws are taped so they can't use
them to hurt their opponents. As a result, the lobsters become depressed and go into a state like hibernation.

A woman in this city buys up lobsters from mar-
kets, drives sixty miles to the ocean, removes the
tape from their claws, and places them in the sea
near a rock jetty. Apparently, they scuttle away to do
whatever it is lobsters do.

Some days I feel emotionally disabled by the ef-
fect of my debts, like one of those poor taped-up
lobsters. The pile of bills on my desk makes me almost unable to breathe, and I feel so guilty and

ashamed I don't want to work or see people. On those days, I'd like to go into hibernation, too. I've got to get untaped and do the things I do best: writing, teaching, enjoying family, getting out into the ocean of life.

For Further Reflection

1. Do you ever feel as if your claws are taped shut, or as if you're crippled emotionally?
2. How is this connected to your debt?
3. What should you ask God to help you do?
4. How can you get back into the swim of life?

Prayer

Help me, Lord. Remove the fetters from my mind and emotions, and let me swim to sea. Amen

Idols on the Shelf

> *Their idols are silver and gold, the work of human*
> *hands. They have mouths, but do not speak; eyes, but*
> *do not see. . . . Those who make them are like them;*
> *so are all who trust in them.*
>
> —Psalm 115:4, 5, 8

There's a legend that Abraham of the Bible worked at his father's idol shop in Babylonia. He helped cast the bronze idols and carved some from wood. A few very rich customers bought figures of gold and silver. Sales were brisk; idols were important in that society, and everyone sacrificed to them.

But one day, Abraham looked around the shelves and said, "How can these figures have any power? I *made* them." The legend says he shattered the idols, then left his home and went across the desert sands, answering the call of the real God, One not made with human hands.

I wonder if I try to give reverence to an idol called Buy It. Instead of turning to God for deep fulfillment, I sometimes put my faith in money and credit and what I can buy. Maybe it's time for *me* to make a trek across the desert until I find out about real sacrifice.

✍ For Further Reflection

Instead of sacrificing your peace of mind to the Buy It idol, sacrifice at the grocery or office supply store in order to pay down an old debt. Shatter your false gods and take away their power.

✍ Prayer

God of Abraham, you alone deserve my worship. Amen

Wilted Flowers

The grass withers, the flower fades; but the word of our God will stand forever.

—Isaiah 40:8

My nine-year-old son was almost in tears. He'd spent most of his allowance for the birthday bouquet he'd bought me at the grocery store—and they wilted the next day. I told him flowers rarely last long and I loved the fact that he'd bought them.

"You could have loved them *longer* if I'd bought plastic ones," he said, still unhappy.

No. I wouldn't have loved them at all. Better real flowers for a day than plastic flowers forever. The daisies and roses and ferns in my son's bouquet were, at least temporarily, celebrations of God's creation, and even when they wilted I could see their colors and breathe their scent. Plastic flowers don't wilt, but from their first day, they shout unreality and have no fragrance.

The abundance of creation is God's handiwork,

while plastic flowers and fake ferns and credit card debt are the inventions of people. Today, I celebrate the choice for God's world instead of purchasing something made by human hands.

For Further Reflection

Spend some time today contemplating things *not* made by hands, and offer your thanks for them.

Prayer

O God, help me not to put my faith in what we make, but in what you ordain. Amen

Certain and Sure

Keep straight the path of your feet, and all your ways will be sure.

—Proverbs 4:26

I walk almost every day, and I rarely vary my route: I take the old logging road behind our house, I pass an abandoned quarry, and I hike up through the Douglas fir trees to the top of the steep hill.

When we first moved to this neighborhood and started walking, I wasn't sure where I was going. I had several near mishaps. I walked across the rocks in the quarry—and heard rattlesnakes! I tried to cut through the vine maple trees at the edge of the wood, and almost stepped on a chickadee's nest. And one dark, cloudy winter day I accidentally went down the wrong side of the hill, and was lost for a while in a meadow I had never seen before.

But now my steps are certain and sure as I walk along. I stick to my route, not because I'm set in my ways but because after my trial-and-error experiments I know it's the best way to go, and the changing seasons make it ever new.

I think getting out of debt will be the same kind of experience. I've made some errors and hit some dead ends, but now that I'm on the right path, I'll stay there.

For Further Reflection

1. What regular, repeated activities make you feel safe and secure?
2. Do you keep trying shortcuts and money-making schemes to get out of debt?
3. How can you find the "straight path" for getting out of debt?

Prayer

Keep my feet on the path, Lord, and guide me to safety. Amen

One, Two, Three, Jump

. . . by my God I can leap over a wall.
    —2 Samuel 22:30

When my grandson was about four, his favorite activity was to stand, on the sofa or a chair, reciting the words, "One, two, three, jump!" Then he would leap out into the room. He got to be a good jumper, and his confidence soared—until the day he stood at the top of a flight of stairs in an office building and repeated those words. Both parents rushed to grab him, but it was too late; he landed on the bottom steps, his knees and nose skinned, and with a lump on his head.

"But it looked easy," he complained.

So does getting online with a bookstore or new website, or visiting my favorite stores downtown—and leaping into yet more credit card debt. And though I don't skin my nose or knees, I certainly feel plenty of pain when bills fill up my mailbox and I have to deplete my bank account to pay them.

For Further Reflection

1. Are you jumping into debt with impulse buying?
2. Can you remember to count 1-2-3-STOP?
3. If you see something you really want, are you willing to wait 48 hours before you buy or order?

Prayer

You are a God of action. Help me know which actions to take. Amen

Curbside Service

*Lazy hands make a man poor, but diligent hands
bring wealth.*

—Proverbs 10:4

Doctors keep warning us that laziness will kill us
all. Remote control devices and automobiles have
replaced walking, and more than half the nation is
overweight. I don't have to go into a store to spend
money: I can drive up to the fast-food window or
the cleaners, and order books or clothes or gifts online. I can hit the ATM machine from the window
of my automobile. Our city even sports one drive-
in church service. Now a finance company in town
says all I have to do is pull up to their window, show
my driver's license and banking information, and
they'll process my loan, on the spot!

I wonder how much of my debt is a result of
laziness? If I had to make a list of things I wanted to
buy, drive downtown or take a bus to the mall, then
look through the stores for everything on my list

and then pay cash, most of the things on my list would look a lot less desirable.

For Further Reflection

For an entire day, do everything the "old" way: Tune your TV by walking to it, cook from scratch, walk anywhere you need to go. Buy everything with cash at a retail store. At the end of the day, examine how you feel about yourself and your money.

Prayer

Lord, you made us able to move our bodies and use our minds. Help me to exercise both. Amen

Cheaters Never Win

> When you make a sale to your neighbor or buy from
> your neighbor, you shall not cheat one another . . .
> for I am the Lord your God.
>
> —Leviticus 25:14, 17

I used to sing-song "Cheaters never wi-in" when I
was a kid. I believed it: My parents said that the
truth would always out, and that someone who
welshed on a trade or swindled in a game would always lose.

But as I grew up, I heard that cheaters *did* sometimes succeed in government or the stock market
or in business. And in every mail delivery, on the
telephone, and in TV commercials, I'm bombarded
with the idea that I can spend a lot more money
than I earn. Which is a form of cheating.

Oh, I eventually pay my bills, or at least pay on
them. I'm not trying to get out of my responsibili-
ties or welsh on my creditors. I'm cheating only *one*
person: me.

I've cheated myself out of serenity and an easier life. I also can't travel, or give to charities I care about, or save for retirement. All I can do is try to keep treading water.

I can change. God will help me quit cheating myself, and then I can win.

For Further Reflection

1. List the ways you cheat yourself: with debt, overeating, smoking, or careless driving.
2. Now make a list of things you'd do if you could afford to.
3. On your third list, note what strategies you're going to use to get out of debt.

Prayer

I don't want to be a cheater, dear God, even against myself. Help me win the battle against debt. Amen

The Pearl of Great Price

Again, the kingdom of heaven is like a merchant in search of fine pearls; on finding one pearl of great value, he went and sold all that he had and bought it.
—*Matthew 13:45, 46*

He could mortgage his house. He might ask for revolving credit or at least ninety-day terms. And if he didn't have loan companies calling him daily, offering low-interest home refinancing, a number of credit opportunities were available, even in the first century. But when he saw the pearl of great value, the wise merchant sold all his other gems and bought it.

Nowadays, people want it all: the amazing pearl, the new five-bedroom house, the SUV *and* the sports car. The message in America today is, *if you want it, get it now.*

Jesus wasn't giving lessons in financial prudence when he told this story; he was talking about the kingdom of heaven. But his secondary message is there for me to find and use as an example of economic caution: *If you want it, be ready to pay for it.*

Advertising urges us to buy into an affluent lifestyle—an in-debt-forever lifestyle. But how can I enjoy my belongings when I owe so much money? I think I see the light, shining like a huge, beautiful white pearl.

✍ For Further Reflection

1. Make a list of things you've been wanting.
2. Put the price beside each one of the items.
3. Choose one of them, and decide how you'll pay *cash* for it: Will you sell something, or save up?

✍ Prayer

Kind Creator, show me what's most important. Amen

Confrontation

Then the Lord said to Moses, "Get up early in the morning, confront Pharaoh and say to him, 'This is what the Lord, the God of the Hebrews, says: Let my people go. . . .'"

—*Exodus 8:20*

I don't have to jump out of the bushes to encounter the king of Egypt, as Moses did. What I have to face is much harder: I have sit down at my desk, get out all my bills, and figure out to the penny how much I owe.

Not thinking about totals—including interest and carrying charges—would be so much easier. I could just glance at the minimum payment due—which they put in a convenient little box at the top of the bill—pay that amount, and ignore the balance. Then stay in debt for the rest of my life.

Confrontations aren't easy, especially when you're facing up to your own mistakes. It's easier to play ostrich and refuse to look at the truth. But God will be my anesthetic for pain, and nothing can equal the feeling of relief that comes after I finally face facts. The balance is overwhelming, but not as dangerous to my life as kidding myself.

For Further Reflection

1. Do you know exactly how much you owe?
2. Are you willing to face the truth?
3. What are you really hiding from? Is it yourself?

Prayer

God of love, strengthen and comfort me as I look at the truth. Amen

Treasure in the Field

*The kingdom of heaven is like treasure hidden in a
field, which someone found and hid; then in his joy
he goes and sells all that he has and buys that field.*
                                                    —Matthew 13:44

The elderly woman and her even more elderly
brother were setting up their yard sale when I ar-
rived. The older man carried a little black leather
trunk out of the garage, a trunk with a leather loop
for hanging it on a stagecoach post. I knew it was
about a hundred years old—and I had to have it.

"How much for the little trunk?" I asked, almost
crossing my fingers.

"Oh? Dollar, I guess," the man said, and my
heart began to throb with avarice. My husband put
the little trunk with the ivory corners into our car
and we started to back out. "Stop the car," I said. I
leapt out and began to dig money from my purse
and jacket pockets. I had $15.76, and I put it in the
hand of the elderly woman.

"That little trunk is worth a lot more than a dollar," I said. "This is all I have with me."

She smiled and said this would be fine, and thanked me for my honesty. I knew I had done the right thing. There's more than one kind of debt in this world.

For Further Reflection

1. Would you have taken the trunk and headed for home?
2. Would that be a kind of dishonesty?
3. Is it fair to take advantage of ignorance or innocence?

Prayer

Keep me free, O God, from the debt of dishonesty. Amen

Riding the Tiger

*I will remove savage beasts from the land, and the
swords will not pass through your country.*
—Leviticus 26:6

Sometimes I wake up in the middle of the night,
feeling as if I were in the jungle with the growling
of wild beasts getting closer and closer. I feel sure
giant tigers with huge sharp teeth are lurking
nearby, ready to gobble me up. And those fierce
striped tigers all bear postage stamps between their
eyes, because they're the bills stacked on the
dresser.

I have to creep up on those wild creatures from
behind, slip a muzzle past those swordlike teeth and
over massive jaws, then grab a chair and start tam-
ing those tigers. Because if I keep hiding from the
truth, one of those debt-tigers might have me for
breakfast. I have to get in control by making a real-
istic schedule of payments and talking openly to
my creditors, who don't really have sharp teeth.

ℬ For Further Reflection

1. What is it about your debt that scares you the most?
2. Which would be the most frightening, ignoring your debts or "muzzling" them?
3. What first steps will you take toward eliminating those debt-tigers?

ℬ Prayer

Lord, help me to gird up and face what scares me the most. Amen

Finding Wonder

> But the angel of the Lord said to him, "Why do you
> ask my name? It is too wonderful."
>
> —Judges 13:18

The retreat leader asked each of us to share what
we thought was awe-inspiring. Most of us responded with *big* things: galaxies, sunsets, oceans,
and mountain tops. But one woman quietly said,
"A newborn baby's little fingernail": something
tiny and yet so perfect, and each one unlike any
other.

A friend of mine said her belief in God started
when, as a small child, she saw her first sand dollar
and felt wonder.

"I *knew* someone had to have drawn that flower
design," she said. "It had to be God."

You have to search for wonder. One of the lies
the world tells is that only what can be traded is
valuable, but nothing I can buy or sell or put on a
shelf is creative or awe-inspiring, nor has anything

else offered to save my soul. Only calling on the wonderful Name of God can do that.

ℬ For Further Reflection

Make a list of things you think are wonderful and awe-inspiring. Then notice what percent of them can be bought or sold, and what percent are either found in nature or in your own God-inspired imagination.

ℬ Prayer

Grant me, dear God, the gifts of wonder and imagination. Amen

The Harry Potter Credit Card

... like a magic stone ... wherever they turn they prosper.

—Proverbs 17:8

If young Harry Potter issued a credit card, it would be magical. As soon as you acquired any debt, the card would by sorcery quickly erase the balance! You could buy whatever you want, take planes all over the world, and give wonderful expensive gifts—all without needing credit for more than a moment.

The idea of magic has always attracted humanity. We love fairy tales about geese that lay golden eggs, cats that wear clothes and can speak, and fairy godmothers who literally turn rags to riches. Wouldn't it be fun if you could pick a new shirt off a tree every day, or open a bottomless money bag when you went to the store?

But what God offers is better than magic. God offers *miracles:* the miracle of life itself, the marvel of intelligence, our amazing ability to love one another, and the wonder of Creation. Gifts no magician could ever duplicate. And through Christ, we have a better credit card: one we can cash in for eternal life.

For Further Reflection

Start a Miracle Journal. Every day, record one miracle you have witnessed, whether it's an unexplained healing, or the fact that you didn't run out of gas when the car said empty, or just the leafing out of new leaves on a tree. Once a week, read through your journal.

Prayer

I know there are miracles all around me, God. Give me eyes to see them. Amen

The Stain

Though you wash yourself with lye and use much soap, the stain of your guilt is still before me, says the Lord God.

—Jeremiah 2:22

I was writing a murder mystery and wanted to know how long a bloodstain would remain in, say, a carpet or mattress. I asked an FBI agent, who invited me to prick my finger and bleed onto a sample of carpet. Then we scrubbed the stain with soap and cold water. After that, he sprayed the carpet piece with luminol. When he turned off the lights, the bloodstain glowed up from the fabric we'd just scrubbed and cleansed.

Sometimes I get such a sense of guilt over my debts that I feel as if a big, rusty smear is spread over my life. A stain that, like the one in the carpet or Lady Macbeth's, I could never get out.

But God doesn't send a heavy load of guilt to someone who is struggling. God doesn't stain me with something that can't be washed out, because God is the Helper, not the Accuser. So no matter what you spray me with, when I'm debt-free I'll be guilt-free, too.

✏ For Further Reflection

Pour some ink or food coloring on a piece of paper, and let it dry. Then write on the paper, "This is my guilt." Burn the paper and thank God for freedom from guilt.

✏ Prayer

You do not heap me with guilt, Lord. Teach me not to do it to myself. Amen

A Rain of Plenty

The Lord will open for you his rich storehouse, the heavens, to give the rain of your land in its season and to bless all your undertakings.

—Deuteronomy 28:12

Children love to play "what if" games: What if it rained money or diamonds? Well, according to the Bible, God *wants* to rain down everything we need: food, clothing, money, jobs, homes, and happiness.

But I haven't always been willing to wait for rain. I've started projects or spent money and then asked God to bless what I've done. I didn't ask God before I bought a car that cost too much and had too high an interest rate; instead, I started praying *after* I was drowning in debt.

So that boils down to whether or not I trust God enough to wait. Enough to fix the old car and drive it a little longer, or keep my computer another year, even though it only has a twenty-gig hard drive instead of a forty-gigger. I guess the answer isn't asking God to get me out of a predicament. The answer is praying for rain.

For Further Reflection

1. Which do you do: wait for God's gifts or run ahead of the rain?
2. What would you really have to give up to live on God's providence and your own good sense?
3. What kind of riches does God want to rain down on you?

Prayer

God, I know you want to provide me with a better life. Teach me to wait. Amen

No Place to Hide

Tell me what you have done; do not hide it from me.

—Joshua 7:19

Some people say that when they get calls from creditors and collectors, and the mail is full of bills, they just let the phone ring or toss the bills into the fireplace. They hide from the world.

But we can't hide from ourselves, and ultimately it's better to face the truth. I had to explain to my creditors that I was unable to pay my balances, but that I had a plan, that I would send them money every month, that I wanted to be open and honest with them. I had decided that whatever I said would be the truth, and what's more important, that's what I would start telling myself. And God helped me escape—not from the truth, but from the pain of honesty.

ℬ For Further Reflection

Add up your bills. Then take a deep breath and look at yourself in the mirror. Slowly but firmly, tell yourself who you owe, and how much, and what you're going to do about it. Repeat this exercise until you can answer the phone and tell the truth.

ℬ Prayer

Dear Lord, give me enough strength to tell myself the truth and be honest with others. Amen

Celtic Crosses

God said, "This is the sign of the covenant that I make between me and you and every living creature that is with you, for all future generations."

—Genesis 9:12

I wear mystery. It's a small silver Celtic cross, with a garnet—my birthstone—in its center and a pin on the back. A Celtic cross is also a knot, one that speaks silently about binding and circling, which suggest both the action of humanity and the action of God in life. Binding is what I take from God and into myself forever; circling is God's protecting, tender presence.

When I compare the mystery of my Celtic knot-cross to the snarl of indebtedness, I clearly see the difference. The sign of my faithfulness and God's grace interweaves and guides me toward heaven; debt just tangles around me and causes chaos in my life.

The knot is woven in a pattern that was famous

long before written language, and its significance is profound, if mysterious. I wear the sweet riddle that makes God's presence shimmer with endless possibility. Some knots set you free, and other knots bind you to sorrow. I'll take the one with God in it.

For Further Reflection

Close your eyes and imagine the knot that describes your life in God. Is it looping and symmetrical and lovely to behold like the one around a Celtic cross, or is it a snarl that's keeping you prisoner? Ask God for a sword to cut through the tangle of your indebtedness.

Prayer

O God, you have created all things perfect, and we are creatures of disorder. Let my life be a sign to a broken world. Amen

Hardwood

Go up to the hills and bring wood and build the
house, so that I may take pleasure in it and be
honored, says the Lord.

—Haggai 1:8

My father was building me a big treehouse, and I
wanted to help. I went down to his basement work-
shop and found some smooth golden boards I
thought would make a beautiful floor. But when I
hauled them out to the big paloverde tree where he
was hammering, he glanced down and shook his
head, smiling.

"That's pine," he said. "We can use it to panel
your walls, but it's too soft for the floor. A floor has
to be strong, to take the stress it gets, so we'll make
it from hardwood."

I'm thankful my own "floor" is made of hard,
stubborn wood, the kind that doesn't splinter or
crack under heavy pressure. Because the base of
my life is Christ, who is "made the sure founda-

tion," not only of the faith but also of each of the faithful. And with his hardwood as my foundation, I can do anything. Even pay off my debts and live a life of true freedom.

For Further Reflection

1. If you were made of wood, what kind would you be?
2. Are you making God or money the foundation of your life?

Prayer

Thank you, Lord, for being the foundation of my life. Amen

School Reunion

The reunion was for anyone who had, within certain years, attended any school in our little Arizona town. I left there when I was eleven, so I hadn't seen most of those people for several decades; and then I saw him.

I couldn't remember ever speaking to him directly—the few haughty Anglo families in that little mining community didn't encourage their children to make friends with Latinos, who were the minority—but I'd had a crush on him since we both started in first grade.

So I felt a lot of guilt as I walked up to the handsome man at the reunion and said, "Hi, Joe. I'm Kris Johnson."

He looked amazed, then reached out and grabbed me in a hug. "I loved you through six

grades of school," he said, with tears in his eyes.
"But my folks would have croaked if they knew I
was smitten with an Anglo girl."

We both *owed* each other a debt created by an
unchristian tradition of elitism, a tradition that val-
ued one kind of person more than another. We repaid each other by sharing lunch at the reunion like
friends, and showing off the pictures of our families.

For Further Reflection

Take a look back through your life. Did you
neglect a friend or treat someone snobbishly?
Can you repay that kind of debt in some way?
If you don't know where that person is, confess your sin and inadequacy to God, and ask
him to send love down to that person.

Prayer

Lord, forgive me for the debts of love I owe. Amen

God's Stubborn Love

*I would feed you with the finest of the wheat, and
with honey from the rock I would satisfy you.*
                                                    —Psalm 81:16

Some theologians would like us to think that suffering and sacrifice are the only gifts God holds out,
and that we should reduce our lives to rags and
ashes to please him.

But in the story of the Prodigal Son, his father
gave him a new gown in exchange for rags, put a
valuable ring on his finger, then arranged a rich
feast for him. In fact, throughout the Bible God offers to satisfy any hunger I experience with spiritual
food, to feed me daily on the finest bread, the fruit
of the vine, honey from hidden sources, and to let
me bask in the sweetness of the land. What God
wants for me is an *abundant* life.

Then where is the element of suffering and sacrifice? In Christ's stubborn and compelling love
from the cross. God said, "I will suffer for you, die

for you, pay your debts for you, so you can have a rich, full life. A feast!"

A life of abundance—and no credit cards, signatures, or mortgages required.

ℬ For Further Reflection

1. Do you realize every day that God is *for* you?
2. What gifts is God holding out to you?
3. How has being in debt warped your view of an abundant life?

ℬ Prayer

Dear God, thank you for all your gifts to me, and for the feast you invite me to eat. Amen

Tourniquet

And if your right hand causes you to sin, cut it off
and throw it away; it is better for you to lose one of
your members than for your whole body to go
into hell.

—Matthew 5:30

"Remember," our emergency medical trainer said.
"If someone has a gushing artery and you have to
use a tourniquet on a limb, the patient will probably lose that arm or leg because circulation is cut
off. So do everything else first to stop the bleeding."

Fortunately, I've never had to put a tourniquet
on anyone, so I've been spared that awful choice.
But what if you're bleeding to death financially?
What if the outflow of payments isn't a trickle but
a gushing wound?

Time for a tourniquet. Yes, I may lose something: not an arm or leg, but the credit cards in my
wallet, the ability to buy on impulse, or the pride
I've felt in picking an expensive gift. I might lose an

admirer, or the chance to invest in a good opportunity.

But a tourniquet ultimately saves a life, and stopping my financial bleeding can keep me from a kind of spiritual death. Better to enter the kingdom maimed than to fall into the fire.

For Further Reflection

1. Do you need to put a tourniquet on your finances?
2. What will you have to give up to do that?
3. Are you willing to live without, in order to live at all?

Prayer

Dear God, I'm bleeding to death financially. Give me the courage to apply a stop. Amen

August

Let there be lights in the dome of the sky to
separate the day from the night; and let them be
for signs and seasons.

—*Genesis 1:14*

In Oregon we have a long rainy season but a dry summer. From late spring to fall, we're flooded with sunshine. Our trees leaf out, our roses bloom, and the hills begin to turn yellow, then tan, then brown. By August, the fire danger in our woods is critical—and I'm tired of so much light. I'm probably the only person in the state who loves the rain.

This is a dangerous time for me. I become restless and want to shop. Like a dieter who knows her trigger foods, I know that in late summer I'll get jittery and prone to spend money. So now around August first, I head for the library and bring home a pile of good books. I try new recipes. I swim at an indoor pool to use up my nervous energy. I pray a lot. And just as I'm about out of ways to keep from shopping, we get our first good fall rain. As the grasses turn green again and the fire danger subsides, I feel like myself again.

Rain in Oregon puts out more than one kind of fire, and I thank God for that grace.

ℬ For Further Reflection

1. Do you have any seasonal "danger periods" of overspending?
2. Are Christmas or other holidays full of the temptation to shop, or to go in debt for things that are too expensive?
3. Are you willing to keep a "spend" diary to track your danger times?
4. What will you do to help yourself get through these times?

ℬ Prayer

Thank you for sunshine and rain, God, because they both create growth. Amen

The Holiday Disease

Blessed is the man who will eat at the feast in the kingdom of God.

—Luke 14:15

No matter how many times I say that in July I'll start buying small gifts, no matter how many times the family agrees that we'll either hand-make adult gifts or limit them to a few dollars, I've always had some kind of disease at Christmas. It starts with a fever—the mental fever that makes department stores look like fairyland, and causes so much brain damage that before I know it, I've spent and charged and gone way beyond the so-called limit for gifts. The disease runs its course until my credit cards are maxed out; and it takes me all year to recover.

I love giving gifts, especially to my children and grandchildren. But this year, the plan *has* to be different if I'm going to get out of debt. My gift to myself will be paying cash for everything. My gifts to friends will be homemade snickerdoodles and fudge. And my gifts to my grandchildren will include toys—but also more of me. On Christmas I'm going to create celebration instead of creating more debt. As the writer Washington Irving said, "Christmas is a season for kindling the fire for hospitality in the hall and the genial flame of charity in the heart."

For Further Reflection

1. Do you spend too much on holiday gifts?
2. What's your real motive for so much generosity?
3. Will your family and friends love you just as much if you buy fewer, less expensive gifts?

Prayer

Lord Jesus, Christmas is the day to celebrate your birth. Help me find new, more creative ways to make the day a feast. Amen

The Wild Heart

*For this people's heart has grown dull, and their ears
are hard of hearing, and they have shut their eyes.*
                                                —Matthew 13:15

When did I quit being the young girl who pressed
wildflowers and identified mushrooms? Now that I
have really wonderful binoculars, how come I
rarely watch the birds anymore? I used to scramble
over the rocks by the river, and look up the botani-
cal names of plants I saw. I learned to freeze against
an oak tree, standing absolutely still as a family of
porcupines passed by. When did I go indoors?
When did I point and click my way into so much
debt, instead of exclaiming over the wonder of a
stream where white water shouts over the stones?
When did I start spending my time and money on
things, instead of delighting in spring flowers and
the trees on city streets?

Whenever I started, now is when I stop. I'm still
a woman who likes to watch birds and raise flow-

ers. Today is the first day of going back to my pre-debt life.

For Further Reflection

1. Have you become a person you didn't want to be?
2. How will you regain the wild heart of your youth?
3. What one act can you perform today to retrieve your pleasure in simple things?

Prayer

Dear God, I temporarily lost the love you gave me for life. Grant me the grace to find it again. Amen

The Beavers and the Pear Tree

*The earth brought forth vegetation: plants yielding
seed of every kind, and trees of every kind bearing
fruit with the seed in it. And God saw that it
was good.*

—Genesis 1:12

My friends live on the banks of a river that tumbles
out of the high country a few miles above them and
down to nourish the emerald-green valley. Their
flower beds border a big vegetable and herb garden,
and orchards where trees bend under their heavy
fruits. My friends sell their produce at a farmer's
market, and they depend on these sales for their income.

One late summer morning, they discovered that
during the night, beavers had felled their fruit-laden
pear tree, eaten all the pears, and gone back to the
river! To add insult to injury, the beavers returned
the following evening and took away the fallen tree.

But my friends said that beavers were in the river

long before people settled on its banks, and you always took the chance you'd have to share your garden with the rest of creation. In fact, when they saw that the animals had not only chopped down the tree but also eaten the fruit, they laughed.

"You can't outrun nature," they said. "And we have enough of everything to share it."

⚘ For Further Reflection

1. Do you share the garden of your life with any other creature, or are you competing?
2. Are you in debt because you're trying to outrun nature or your neighbors?
3. Could you laugh if something took one of your possessions away?

⚘ Prayer

Dear God, make me more willing to share, and less determined to possess. Amen

Storm Warning

It will be a shelter and shade from the heat of the day, and a refuge and hiding place from the storm and rain.

—Isaiah 4:6

At ten in the morning, I heard a siren and knew a tornado had set down somewhere nearby. The noise was insistent, and so was the fierce wind outside, so I locked up the shop where I was working and headed for the shelter in the basement of the mall. I had heard tornado warnings on the radio earlier, so I'd parked my car underground to protect it from the massive hail and wind that could accompany such a storm.

I'm not a fool. When I hear a storm siren, I take precautions. Now, another storm is brewing. This one is financial, and the warning is the pile of bills on my desk. What's more, any minute now, that "storm warning" could become a loud siren in my life.

But I don't want to wait until the tempest is upon me. With God as my storm shelter, I'll find a way not only to pay my bills but also to avoid running up any more. I don't want to be a fool about money, either.

⌾ For Further Reflection

Have your debts achieved storm status? Before they blow the roof off your home or batter your life any further, take sensible steps to ward off the tempest.

⌾ Prayer

Lord Jesus, you calmed the wind and stilled the waves. Help me quell a tempest I created. Amen

Work Ethic

By the seventh day God had finished the work he had been doing: so on the seventh day he rested from all his work.

—Genesis 2:2

Lately, all I've been able to do is work. I had several writing deadlines to meet, almost all on the same date, so for a couple weeks I ate lunch—and sometimes even dinner—at my desk. I worked again in the evening and fell into bed with my mind still typing. Though I love my work, I wasn't having much fun doing it.

And then one day, my eleven-year-old grandson asked why I was going home from church to work.

"I need the money," I said.

"Well, but even God rested," he said, and with a sudden burst of inner light, I knew he was right, and I went out to lunch with the family instead of working.

What does all this have to do with debt?

A debtor's life is an unbalanced one. I spend and then I work to pay for what I've bought. Both are a kind of "binge" behavior. For years, my husband has told me I was a workaholic; now, for the first time, I thought maybe he was more right than he knew.

For Further Reflection

1. Are you addicted to spending?
2. Are you also addicted to your work?
3. How can you better balance your life?
4. How much *rest* do you have scheduled into your life?

Prayer

God, teach me how to balance my life. Amen

The Prayer of the Weaver

My frame was not hidden from you, when I was being made in secret, intricately woven in the depths of the earth.

—Psalm 139:15

Have you ever watched someone weave? First he or she has to warp the loom by threading and fastening yarn or thread, then weaving colored strands across it. The warp creates the up-and-down part of fabric, and the weave, or weft, is horizontal thread that creates pattern and texture.

Weaving is hard work. You have to constantly tighten and straighten, to create selvedges, and your vocabulary has to include words like "heddle" and "drawing-in."

Before the weaver trims and cuts the work from the loom, the underside looks messy, with hanging threads and knots. Sometimes I think my debt-filled life looks just as untidy or confused. But then I see the "right" side, the one God sees: I'm a woman making every effort to pay her creditors and live on a cash basis. When I warp the loom of my life with prayer and action, the "right" side is always full of color and a unique pattern.

ℬ′For Further Reflection

1. If your debts were a rug or tapestry, what color would it be?
2. How has working to get out of debt changed that tapestry?
3. Today, use crayons or paints to make a picture of that weaving.

ℬ′Prayer

Lord, help me remember that you will help me create beautiful patterns in my life. Amen

Deep Breath

By the word of the Lord were the heavens made,
their starry host by the breath of his mouth.

—Psalm 33:6

Everything in the universe contains some stardust, scientists tell us. When God set the lights in the heavens as "signs to mark seasons and days and years," the swirling dust of the universe settled into the very bones of our bodies.

And in the same way, the breath of God keeps me and the rest of the creatures on this planet alive. Yet today, I feel so overcome by debt, so depressed by my inability to avoid the temptations of the world, I can hardly make my lungs inflate.

Everything in me is longing—not for money or the things that money can buy, but for grace and joy. The kind of life I can find only in God. A respite from work and freedom from worry. A vacation from struggle. A deep breath.

With God as my help, I will soon breathe free again, and remember that I have stars in my bones.

For Further Reflection

1. When did you last take a deep, long, satisfying breath?
2. How would getting out of debt help you breathe more easily?
3. Do you remember, every day, that you have God's breath in you?

Prayer

God my Creator, you filled me with the breath of life and the dust of stars. Thank you. Amen

Mortgaged Spirit

Take my yoke upon you and learn from me . . . For my
yoke is easy and my burden is light.

—Matthew 11:29, 30

The President was scheduled to speak on the TV
news channel this evening. During the half hour I
waited, I heard one commercial after another, urg-
ing listeners to take out a loan worth more than the
value of their homes, to use their department store
credit cards to earn airline miles, to call *now* to take
advantage of a super sale on the bird clock I've ad-
mired—all on credit. Now that I'm facing up to
debt, I hear the real message in those commercials.
They're saying, *Have it all, now. Don't worry about the*
consequences.

By the time the President came on the screen, I
felt as if advertisers wanted to mortgage more than
my house. They wanted my soul and spirit!

I've always thought "selling your soul to the
devil" was just a common phrase; now I can see

clearly the hell that debt can make in my life. But now I've been in the wilderness and resisted temptation. Sure, I was tempted to add to my airline miles and to buy the bird clock, but I didn't. And I got an amazing reward: My husband came home with a bird clock for me!

For Further Reflection

1. Has the world tried to mortgage your spirit?
2. What are your greatest temptations?
3. How have you learned to resist them?

Prayer

Thank you, Lord, for helping me resist a mortgage on my soul. Amen

Swallows

> Even the stork in the heavens knows its times; and
> the turtledove, swallow, and crane observe the time
> of their coming; but my people do not know the
> ordinance of the Lord.
>
> —Jeremiah 8:7

They come to our property every year, at the end of March; and at least one pair makes its nest under the eaves of our garage. For a few months, when anyone goes outside during the nesting time, the swallows swoop down, warning us that we're on their holy ground and should leave immediately. For most of summer, the swallows are a part of our lives.

Nobody tells swallows or geese or robins when to arrive and when to go; they can't read the clock or the calendar, but they "observe the time of their coming," and of their leaving again.

They are absolutely obedient to nature, which means they follow God's laws. I think birds and wolves and seals know God the same way the angels do: God commands, and they obey with love.

What does this have to do with being in debt? God has said to owe no one anything. Now, shall I behave like birds and beasts and angels, or like other sinful humans?

For Further Reflection

1. Decide whether you want to obey God completely.
2. Ask God to take over your money.
3. Listen for instructions.

Prayer

Lord, you made us in your image and gave us the breath of life. Teach us how to put our faith not in our walls, but in our wings. Amen

Baked Goods

So Abraham hurried into the tent to Sarah. "Quick"
he said, "get three seahs of fine flour and knead it
and bake some bread."

—Genesis 18:6

Today I felt deprived: I wanted to go out for dinner,
but I'd used all my spare money to pay bills. Then I
remembered being in a Near Eastern city, with a
group of small, ragged boys trotting beside me.
They all held out their hands and said the same
word. At first I thought they were saying "money,"
because the country is full of beggars. Until that
day, I had believed that anyone who begs for money
should get a job.

The crowd of kids was growing, and pressing
closer against me. I got out my phrase book and finally found the word they were chanting. *Bread.*

Soon we came to a bakery, and after I had
bought enough round, flattish bread for every child
to have a loaf—costing a total of $5—I handed

them out. The boys snatched them and ran away, shouting and laughing, pinching off pieces of bread and gobbling them.

Tonight at dinner, we had a simple meal with grape juice and a loaf of my hot homemade bread. Communion.

For Further Reflection

Spend some time today thinking about the importance of bread in the history of the world, and in Christian life. Then make a loaf of bread and serve it to your household or friends.

Prayer

Lord of heaven and earth, give us today our daily bread. Amen

Night Song

*By day the Lord commands his steadfast love, and at
night his song is with me, a prayer to the God of
my life.*

—Psalm 42:8

I did everything I knew of to help me sleep. I drank
herbal tea and took a warm bath. I lay in the dark
and counted my breaths. I only did that as long as I
could, and then, as usual, my mind wandered to my
money problems. In just moments, I was in an anxiety state. I prayed mightily: I begged God to release
me from my disquiet, to grant me tranquility, to let
me sleep. But I felt as if my prayers went no higher
than the ceiling, and pretty soon, my stomach was
in a knot.

Finally, I got up and wandered out to the living
room. A new hymnal lay on the stand of my piano,
and I sat down to leaf through it. Before I knew it,
I was singing "Praise to the Lord, the almighty, the
king of creation . . ."

I sang hymns of exaltation for about fifteen minutes, and then I was so sleepy that I shuffled back and fell in bed. Instead of begging God for comfort, I had sung praises. And instead of dwelling on my debts, I had put my focus on the One who will help me pay them off.

For Further Reflection

1. Are you staying awake at night, or making yourself nervous during the day, because of debt?
2. When you pray, is money and debt what you pray about?
3. Are you willing to let God plan your future?

Prayer

Praise you, O God; I magnify your holy Name. Amen

Up the Waterspout

Gentiles, who did not strive for righteousness, have attained it, that is, righteousness through faith.
                                                    —Romans 9:30

I always took the song about the eentsy-weentsy spider to heart, believing I had to bail myself out of my own problems. If life washed me down the waterspout, I was supposed to shake the water off my arms and legs and climb upward again.

But life taught me a few lessons. I had pneumonia and spent more than a week in an oxygen tent, unable to breathe on my own. After I broke my shoulder I couldn't put my carry-on bag into the overhead compartment without help from the flight attendant. And when someone violated my copyright, I had to consult a lawyer with expertise in that field.

Despite these lessons, I thought I had to get out of debt on my own. Like the eentsy-weentsy spider, I kept trying to climb up the slippery waterspout all alone. Now it's time to turn to the experts. Financial consultants. And God.

For Further Reflection

1. Do you pride yourself on being "self-reliant"?
2. Do pride and what you mistake for self-respect keep you from getting help?
3. What kinds of help do you need to get out of debt?

Prayer

Remind me every day, God, that you—not I—direct the universe. Amen

Stand Fast and Reply

By standing firm you will gain life.
—Luke 21:19

I once lived near the country's biggest navy helicopter base, and one afternoon I hiked over to have a quick cup of coffee with a friend who worked in the base commissary. As I neared the sentry gate, a sign read, "Stand fast and reply."

In a moment, a nearby speaker box repeated those same words, then asked who I was and what I wanted. Still standing fast—in fact, trembling a little—I announced my name and the purpose of my visit, and soon the gate opened. I never did see the sentry, but the phrase "Stand fast and reply" continued to ring in my head.

Maybe God is telling me to stop, stand firm, square my shoulders and say who I am, and what my errand is on earth. Is it to live on the brink of financial disaster, or to have life abundant? Today, I have ready the right reply: I'm getting out of debt.

For Further Reflection

1. If you heard God's voice right now, what would it be saying?
2. Can you stand still and proudly tell God your name and where you are in your struggle?

Prayer

You are the sentry in my life, God. Teach me freedom from debt. Amen

New Fire

Do not put out the Spirit's fire.
—1 Thessalonians 5:19

Every year our church holds a vigil on the night before Easter. The service begins outside, at night, when we light the "new fire" of Eastertide. The service marks the end of Lent and winter and sadness, and the beginning of a fresh, more celebratory kind of season. Darkness and cold are about over. And so are fasting and gloominess.

When I look back over the years of being in debt, I feel as if I'd been dead inside all that time. Instead of enjoying the people and events around me, I've worked and worked to pay my bills—and then created more.

Easter is the season of resurrection, the time of rising from death, a time of joy and promise. Now it's time to think about lighting a new fire for myself. I want to rise from the ashes of debt. I don't want to stay in the same old spend-owe-pay-interest season that strips me of joy and freedom; I want to live a celebration of life, a life with peace of mind.

Maybe I'll start the new fire with my old credit cards.

For Further Reflection

1. Is there any part of your life that needs resurrecting?
2. What steps can you take to light the "new fire"?
3. How will your new life look different from your old one?

Prayer

Light new fire within me, O Christ, and give me new life. Amen

The Little Engine

I press on toward the goal to win the prize for which God has called me heavenward in Christ Jesus.
—Philippians 3:14

"What changed my life," the successful woman told me, "was a gift from a friend. I was miserable, going through divorce, my kids were in trouble, I was up to my neck in debt, and I was sleeping half the day, just so I didn't have to face reality. And then my friend sent me that book and after I read it, I felt strong enough to stand up and solve my problems."

What is that wonder book that can change lives? A text on psychology, or a great religious work? No, it was *The Little Engine That Could*, the children's classic by Watty Piper. The book contains those famous lines we all grew up with: "I think I can, I think I can, I think I can. . . ."

How many lives has that book changed? How many of us today need to read those words again, and take heart as we strive toward the goal?

I'm getting out of debt. Almost up the hill. With God's help, I know I can, I know I can.

✍ For Further Reflection

Get a copy of *The Little Engine That Could*, by Watty Piper, and read it aloud to yourself. Then start thinking, "I think I can."

✍ Prayer

I'm sure I can, Lord. Just give me a push from behind. Amen

Not Good Enough

Answer me quickly, O Lord; my spirit fails. Do not hide your face from me or I will be like those who go down to the pit.

—Psalm 143:7

At the end of a retreat I attended, several of the women stood to talk about what they'd gained in the three days, or to tell how their viewpoint was changed, or to express their excitement about the future. Finally, one tall, rawboned woman stood and, while staring at her feet, thanked us for a wonderful retreat.

"I didn't believe . . . I mean, I thought I wasn't good enough for God . . ." she began, and our groans echoed throughout the church. We sighed with sorrow not only for our shy, gentle sister who finally revealed that she had been beaten and abused by her parents; we also groaned for ourselves, because she was reciting the feelings of every woman there. No matter whether we had abusive parents or lived in palaces, most of us feel as if we don't measure up.

Being a debtor makes that feeling worse. The tapes that play in my head say, "Not good enough . . . can't do anything right . . . failure, failure, failure. . . ."

Thank God for that other voice, the still, small voice that whispers, "Well done, good and faithful servant."

For Further Reflection

Write today in your journal all the feelings you have about not being good enough, not making the mark, about being a failure. Then ask God to heal those feelings.

Prayer

Lift me up, God, for today my spirit is low. Amen

Storehouse of Treasures

*Do not store up for yourselves treasures on earth,
where moth and rust consume and where thieves
break in and steal; but store up for yourselves
treasures in heaven.*

—Matthew 6:19, 20

Wild roses tumble over our hillsides in spring,
scenting the air and calling bees out of their hives.
In fall, those same rosebushes bear bright red
rose hips, full of nutrients for the plant, seeds for
more rosebushes—and the makings of wonderful
dark red jelly. The rose blossom stores up energy
from the sun and rain to form the round, crimson
"rose apples" that contain seeds for next year's
plants. A rose hip is full of promise, a storehouse of
roses.

What am I storing up? Books? Clothes? CDs?
Electronics? Those expensive belongings won't
make me fit for the Kingdom of God. Just as the
rose hip is a storehouse of roses, so I can become a

storehouse of prayer. Treasure in heaven is free, and everlasting.

Eventually the plump, bright rose hips begin to darken and shrivel, but prayer is *always* fresh and whole and full of promise. And won't put me in debt.

ᗌ For Further Reflection

1. Which of your belongings do you consider to be "treasure"?
2. What treasure have you stored in heaven?
3. This week, every time you're tempted to buy something, pray instead.

ᗌ Prayer

Teach me your values, dear God, and turn me into a storehouse of prayer. Amen

Coffee Break

The Lord himself goes before you and will be with
you; he will never leave you nor forsake you. Do not
be afraid; do not be discouraged.

—Deuteronomy 31:8

Changing the mood in a room isn't too hard. A per-
fumed candle, fresh flowers, or some bright-
colored throw cushions can completely alter a
space's feeling. Today, as my coffee grinder whirred,
the fragrance of roasted beans suffused my clean,
empty kitchen. Suddenly the cold winter morning
was transformed, and the quiet room was filled
with a celebratory spirit. As I sipped the rich, hot
beverage, I thought about how much difference a
spoonful of coffee beans could make in the ambi-
ence of a room.

The same is true about getting out of debt.
Once in a while, I can make a big payment; but just
a penny or quarter or dollar that I put toward debt
repayment changes the balance—and the mood—

of our household. Just as the ocean can wear away a rocky shoreline, so my small economies can erase the red ink in our budget.

And one of these days, the house will be brighter and happier because we'll be debt-free. Meanwhile, I'll keep grinding those coffee beans, making winter mornings more like a party, with the assurance that God won't desert me while I'm struggling.

For Further Reflection

Do something small, something that costs nothing, to change the mood in your house. Simmer some cloves in water on your stove, or tie your curtains back with a string of beads, or play classical music while you eat dinner. Express your gratitude to God for change.

Prayer

You made me to be creative and joyful, Lord. Forgive me for despair. Amen

Polonius

My mouth speaks what is true, for my lips detest
wickedness.

—Proverbs 8:7

In Shakespeare's *Hamlet*, the courtier Polonius
counsels his son Laertes—brother of Ophelia—
about behavior: Don't act before you think; dress
like a gentleman; be familiar but not vulgar; listen
more than you speak; don't borrow or lend, be careful of friendship. He ends his discourse by saying,

> *This above all: to thine own self be true,*
> *And it must follow, as the night the day,*
> *Thou canst not then be false to any man.*

What does this mean? How do I apply it to my
situation?

Here's the answer: If I am true to myself, then
I'll be truthful with everybody else. Including my
creditors.

This means if I hold my faith in God pure, keep my accounts honest, and do what I say I will, *I can be trusted*. That's a big step for a debtor, because when our bills are overdue, we feel guilty and unworthy of trust. Today, I am reliable!

For Further Reflection

1. Are you really true to yourself?
2. Do you pretend you're someone you're not?
3. Can you be trusted?

Prayer

Make me an instrument of truth, Lord. Teach me to be trustworthy. Amen

A Beggar on the Corner

I tell you the truth, whatever you did for one of the least of these brothers of mine, you did for me.

—Matthew 25:40

She stands on the corner where I turn to go to church. Her sign says, "Hungry, disabled, God bless you." Because she has to lean on her cane with both hands, she carries a bag around her waist to catch the contributions from passersby. She has rheumatoid arthritis, so she's always cold, her thin, small body wrapped in several layers, including a hooded jacket.

She can no longer work because of her twisted hands and crooked legs. She receives some disability, but it's not enough. Her tiny apartment costs too much, her falling-apart car always needs repairs, and then there's the debt she's faithfully paying off. Once when she was living in her car, her brakes released while she slept, and the car slid downhill into another vehicle. She's paying for the damage at the rate of ten dollars a week.

I give her some of my tithe every week, and sometimes I take her to lunch or dinner. This impoverished woman can smile at traffic and pay off what she owes; maybe my financial problems aren't so overwhelming.

For Further Reflection

Do you see someone with a sign as you go through your week? Make an effort to know about the situation, and find out how you can help. Knowing such a person may help you face your own indebtedness.

Prayer

Remind me, God, that what I give away belongs to you anyway. Amen

Grandmother Wisdom

Bring the whole tithe into the storehouse, that there may be food in my house.

—Malachi 3:10

My grandmother, who was four-feet-ten and weighed seventy pounds, taught me two basic religious precepts. The first was that you might choke to death on unblessed food, so you should always thank God for your meal; and the second was that if you tithe, God will make sure you always have enough to live on and are able to pay your bills.

Nana tithed all her life. I never heard her say she couldn't afford something; I never saw the day when she didn't have a little money for a grandchild or great-grandchild. In her last years, she faithfully tithed her Social Security and railroad pension, and lived out her days without wanting for anything.

The last time I saw her, she had just come home from church, where she paid her weekly tithe. "I feel as if I've already gone to heaven," she said, and

she died in her sleep a few weeks later, owing nobody anything, and with God paid in full.

For Further Reflection

1. Are you waiting until you're out of debt to
   tithe?
2. Do you trust God to take care of you if you
   give more to the church and the poor?
3. What percentage of your *time* do you give
   to God's work?

Prayer

Show me how you want me to use my money, dear
God, and where to put my tithe. Amen

Spare Tire

*Fear not, O land; be glad and rejoice for the Lord
will do great things.*

—Joel 2:21

I had a flat tire about fifty miles from home. In my
car's four-year lifetime, I had never had to change a
tire until then. When my roadside service man
opened my trunk, he took out what looked like the
wheel for a little red wagon, and I was scared.

"My car will list to one side! It'll veer off the
highway!" I cried, but he explained that the tiny
spare would get me home just fine, and the car
would remain balanced. He was right, but as soon
as I was in town, I headed for the shop and had my
original tire repaired.

The budget I'm running on now is a lot like that
midget-sized spare. Most of our income is going to
debt repayment, and we don't have room for many
indulgences or foolishness. But our small household allowance is buying food and paying the mort-

gage, keeping us upright and balanced, so I guess it's okay.

One day we'll have our finances repaired and we'll be on a full-sized budget. But for right now, our financial "spare tire" is working out just fine.

✍ For Further Reflection

Are you still spending and charging, or are you on a "spare tire" budget? Make a list of things you have to have, such as rent, food, and utilities, and start using anything left over for debt repayment.

✍ Prayer

Creator of heaven and earth, help me discern what I need and what I can use to get out of debt. Amen

Vulture Drill

They fly like a vulture swooping to devour.
                                        —Habakkuk 1:8

Most people think of vultures as ugly, greedy, and sure to lose any popularity contest. With their bare heads and long curved necks, vultures do appear repulsive as they clamor around dead animals, waiting for the first opportunity to feast on carrion. Yet, in spite of their bad reputation, vultures serve a useful and necessary purpose in the natural world. They clear away dead and rotting flesh to make way for all things new.

I used to think of my credit card debt as a greedy vulture, swooping down to devour my cash and my peace of mind. Those plastic cards were everywhere, waiting for my willpower to falter. The credit vultures could then feast on my weaknesses, raking in the interest.

As I begin to crawl out from under my debt load, I no longer fear the vultures. Paying down my debts each and every month may not be pretty or popular, but it's clearing away a mountain of dead weight in my life. I'm going to drill myself to pounce on my bills like a vulture, instead of sitting helplessly while debt consumes me.

For Further Reflection

1. Do you think of your debts as vultures, waiting to consume your life?
2. Are you willing to become a "vulture," constantly scanning for creeping debt?

Prayer

Teach me to be alert, Lord, and to swoop down on my bills. Amen

Financial Fitness

You must be mentally stripped for action, perfectly self-controlled.

—1 Peter 1:13

The aerobics instructor barked out orders like a drill sergeant. "One more set," she commanded, and the class groaned in unison. I knew I'd be sore for a week but I pushed myself, knowing that if I stuck it out I'd be rewarded with a trimmer, healthier body.

After that first class, every muscle in my body urged me to drop out. Yet each time I felt like quitting, I imagined the new physically fit me. After a few weeks, I could keep up with that instructor and exercise got much easier. These days I look forward to aerobics.

A strict budget is like going back to that exercise class. Living within one's means takes determination and commitment—especially when the going gets tough. I can make all the resolutions I want, but if I give up after the first few painful tries at fitness, I won't reap the benefits of better financial health. I'm going to keep imagining the new financially fit me—and make a habit of exercising a sensible budget.

For Further Reflection

1. Are you financially fit?
2. What first steps can you take to be "stripped for action"?
3. What first exercise do you need to do?

Prayer

I'm out of shape, Lord. Help me to get spiritually and financially fit. Amen

Is Less Really More?

For to me, to live is Christ and to die is gain.
—*Philippians 1:21*

All my problems would be solved, I thought, if only I had enough money. I'd be able to live in a nice house, drive a better car, and buy all the things my family ever wanted.

Then I read some stories about people who had won millions in state lotteries. One man squandered his fortune in a year and was living on the streets. Another family fought bitterly over the prize money and no longer spoke to each other. Yet another single woman who won the jackpot found herself hounded by greedy suitors. She claimed she was much happier when she was just a clerk in a convenience store.

Everyone can fall into the trap of believing riches bring happiness. But money can create as many problems as it solves, and sometimes less is more. I've stopped dreaming about hitting the jackpot and I'm buying only what I need.

And now I smile at every convenience store clerk I meet.

✍ For Further Reflection

1. Do you still think money alone could solve all your problems?
2. What other factors—boredom, loneliness, anxiety—drove you into debt?
3. How can you change that?

✍ Prayer

Thank you, God, for showing me what is important. Amen

Facing Fear

Do not be afraid; do not be discouraged. Be strong and courageous.

—Joshua 10:25

When threatened by another animal, an opossum plays dead. By rolling on its back and remaining perfectly still, the opossum often fools its enemy into thinking it isn't worth eating. But sometimes the plan backfires. The predator hides nearby and pounces when the opossum gets up again, thinking the coast is clear.

I'm acting like an opossum when I try to hide from my creditors. When the bills pile up, it's tempting to play dead and ignore the people I owe. I'm scared because I can't pay the whole amount and so I pay nothing. I stay perfectly still, doing nothing, hoping the bills will eventually get tired and go away. I try not to think about how those debts may suddenly pounce on me, just as I think the coast is clear.

I don't have to "play possum" in order to climb out of debt. Although I may be discouraged by the large amount I owe, I can decide to pay something every month, without fail. It takes courage to pay off a bill little by little but I can do it.

For Further Reflection

1. Are you trying to hide from the truth about your money situation?
2. Why are you afraid of the truth—or are you afraid of *someone*?
3. What will it take to make you uncurl, open your eyes, and face reality?

Prayer

Your way is the way of honesty, dear Jesus. Show it to me. Amen

Wolf in Sheep's Clothing

Beware of false prophets, which come to you in sheep's clothing, but inwardly they are ravening wolves. Ye shall know them by their fruits.
—Matthew 7:15, 16

Credit cards now come in gold, platinum, even titanium. Every week I get a different offer in the mail. Even the cards I already hold urge me to upgrade to a better rate or a higher limit. If I ignore the mail offers, I get phone calls from salespeople who promise extra perks if I'll only sign up for one more credit line.

The pitch sounds good. A higher limit will make me feel more important. I tell myself I might need a card with more clout in case of emergency. And what could be better than titanium? Still, I wonder why these companies are wooing me, instead of the other way around. Are they really interested in helping me, or are they lying in wait, ready to make a profit from my spending habits?

Credit cards can be disguised wolves at the door. I need to make sure my own desires aren't the real wolves in my life. Today I won't be taken in by gold, platinum, or even titanium.

For Further Reflection

Save all the offers for credit cards and loans you get in a month. Then use them to make a small bonfire that keeps the wolves from your door!

Prayer

Guard me from temptation, Lord. Amen

Ladder out of the Mud

They lowered Jeremiah by ropes into the cistern, it had no water in it, only mud, and Jeremiah sank down into the mud.

—Jeremiah 38:6

When the monthly statement comes, it always lists a minimum payment due. I used to think my creditors were being kind by not requiring payment in full.

"They must know I'm on a budget," I thought. "They're only asking me for twenty dollars this month."

Then I did a little arithmetic. I calculated that by paying only the minimum on a balance, I ended up forking over nearly double the original price of an item. I could keep sending these small amounts, racking up the interest indefinitely. And the companies would be happy to let me do it. What I thought was a nice gesture was really a way to keep me sinking into the mud of debt.

I no longer wish to take one step forward and fall two back on the ladder of revolving accounts. Buying on credit is convenient and sometimes necessary, but I can take charge. From now on, I'm going to pay off my bills as quickly as possible, and keep interest down.

For Further Reflection

1. Are you making minimum payments on credit cards?
2. Which bills carry the highest interest?
3. Are you willing to go without something so you can make bigger payments?

Prayer

I feel as if I'm sinking in mud or quicksand, God. Give me wisdom to climb upward. Amen

Plain Speech

*Let your gentleness be evident to all. The Lord
is near.*

—Philippians 4:5

The Society of Friends' John Woolman (1720–1772)
experienced conversion in early childhood, but
during his teens he said, "I found in myself great
danger." At twenty-one, when he was a shop-
keeper and accountant, he wrote in the first chapter
of the book we know as his *Journal*, "After a while,
my former acquaintances gave over expecting
me as one of their company, and I began to be
known to some whose conversation was helpful
to me."

That "conversation" was *encouragement*. Woolman was striving to be merciful, tender, and gentle
to people and animals, and he needed help. As
we all do. Without the encouragement of a few
friends, I wouldn't even be trying to get out of debt.
I don't need someone to manage my life, and I

don't want a steady dose of advice; but I do need to be able to call a friend when I stumble.

The Quakers spoke to one another as "thee," to show equality and friendship. They called this "Plain Speech," which is the kind of talk we need to hear when we're climbing out of the debt pit.

ℬ'For Further Reflection

Do you have a close friend who's a cheering section in your struggle with debt? If not, look around your church and ask God to show you the person who could be your encourager.

ℬ'Prayer

Thank you, God, for friends. Amen

Making a Decision

Stand at the crossroads and look; ask for the ancient paths, ask where the good way is, and walk in it, and you will find rest for your souls.

—Jeremiah 6:16

Decisions aren't always easy for me. Although I'm determined *after* I come to a conclusion, I don't find the process easy. Since getting out of debt means choosing how to do it, I had to decide: Should we take out a consolidation loan, get financial counseling, declare bankruptcy, just bite the bullet and go without things while we paid off the high-interest credit cards, or what?

Finally my husband said, "Well, we could always do the most desperate thing first."

"What?" I said. "You mean—declare bankruptcy? I don't think that's—"

"No, I mean *pray*," he said, laughing. So we did. We prayed and prayed, and soon our answer looked clear.

Even then, I had to make sure we could live with the solution, which was to go on a severe austerity program and start making double payments on everything. So we slept on our decision and in the morning, over coffee, we prayed again. Now we're living with our resolve, and we think God is in that decision.

ℬ For Further Reflection

1. Pray for guidance.
2. List all the ways you might get out of your financial predicament.
3. Pray again, and ask God to show you the best path.
4. Follow your answer.

ℬ Prayer

Thank you for guidance, Lord, and for the path to freedom. Amen

Good News

How beautiful on the mountains are the feet of those who bring good news.

—Isaiah 52:7

What if people with balloons and a giant check for ten million dollars came to my door? According to television commercials, all that's required is that I send in a contest entry.

Not far from my home is a billboard that tells what the latest lottery figure is, and it's up to eighty-one million. All I'd have to do is buy a lottery ticket.

Or imagine this scenario: I open the afternoon newspaper and read this headline: "Your debts have been paid by an anonymous donor." I just need to do a good deed to a stranger, and he or she will reward me with a fortune.

Well, prospects for any of those events are poor. But good news *is* on the horizon: God will give anyone who asks the strength and wisdom to solve problems. When I move forward one step, God, working behind the scenes, carries me a few more.

And I don't have to buy a lottery ticket or send in an entry.

For Further Reflection

1. Are you waiting for the lottery or a sudden windfall to solve your money problems?
2. How likely is that to happen?
3. Can you believe God is helping you?
4. Are you willing to keep trying?

Prayer

Lord Jesus, you gave me the great miracle of salvation. Help me look for answers, not magic. Amen

Sending Out the Raven

After forty days Noah opened the window he had
made in the ark.

—Genesis 8:6

Whatever made Noah send out a *raven*, for heaven's sake? He could have sent out an albatross, which can fly for thousands of miles without landing; or he could have dropped a hippo or alligator into the ocean and let it swim beside the craft as it teetered on a peak of Mt. Ararat. Instead, he pushed a poor raven out the window, and it flew to and fro, most likely landing on the ark's roof for a rest, then taking off again.

In ancient times, long before they were immortalized in Edgar Allan Poe's poem, ravens were symbols of dark prophecy, of death, pestilence, and disease. I suspect Noah was pretty depressed when he picked a bird with such a bad reputation. In fact, I think Noah had actually lost hope that he'd ever get off the ark. But God had not abandoned him, and in a few more days, the dove he released brought back an olive twig.

A few months ago, I was about ready to send out a raven. I felt hopeless and gloomy and saw no way out of my problem. But each day I stay with my plan, the sea of my debt is receding, and who knows? Maybe I'll soon be ready to send out my dove.

✍ For Further Reflection

In your journal, write down the bird or animal or reptile that represents your emotional state right now. If your choice is sad and droopy, or mean and dangerous, talk to someone about your depression. It's okay to ask for help.

✍ Prayer

God, some days I can hardly open a window, much less release a bird. Help! Amen

Mystery Weekend

And he made known to us the mystery of his will according to his good pleasure, which he purposed in Christ.

—Ephesians 1:9

Some years ago I went with a close friend to a Murder Mystery Weekend. We didn't know which of the people in the little hotel were guests like ourselves and which were actors in the mystery, so we ate together and socialized, constantly scrutinizing one another to solve the crime.

On the last morning at breakfast, we turned in our written solutions to our "tour guide." I was amazed and delighted when he awarded me first prize for solving the puzzle and naming the murderer; he said nobody else had discerned every single clue the way I had (in fact, my friend won the booby prize). My award was an attractive ceramic wall hanging—the face of Humphrey Bogart, wearing a typical film noir slouch hat, about sixteen inches high.

I hung Humphrey over the window in my little home office, but not so I would continue to feel triumphant or to make my friend humble. Nor did I hang it up so people would ask about it, meaning I could brag, even though that occasionally happens. My main reason for displaying the prize is to remind myself that *nothing* is too hard for me to figure out. Not even my bills.

For Further Reflection

Do you ever feel as if debt and credit are mysterious and impossible to figure out? Approach them like a mystery novel, and maybe you'll find an answer.

Prayer

God of the universe, you have the answers to all mysteries. Help me with mine. Amen

Harsh Words

A gentle answer turns away wrath but a harsh word stirs up anger.

—Proverbs 15:1

My husband and I wake up differently. He springs out of bed, able to balance a checkbook or make a series of business phone calls, while I crawl out barely able to turn on lights or let the dog out.

So early this morning, when he asked me to look at a bill and identify the expenditure before I had a cup of coffee, I was surly. He responded with annoyance, and in a few minutes we were almost shouting. I began to think bad thoughts: *I'll wait until this evening, when he's half asleep and I'm feeling bouncy, and then I'll get even. I'll—*

But I didn't get even, which is never satisfying. We ate breakfast in silence, and then we began to talk about the Middle East situation, and then the front lawn, and finally we got back to the bill, and the day smoothed out.

Not everyone is so lucky. Marriages have broken down under a pile of bills, and debt can destroy a relationship if you let it.

For Further Reflection

1. Is your indebtedness affecting any relationships in your life?
2. How can you change that?

Prayer

Thank you for making me able to love, God. Now help me love all the time. Amen

Calling Crows

You will drink from the brook and I have ordered
the ravens to feed you there.

—1 Kings 17:4

My friend Mike was reading a seed-and-gardening catalogue in bed. When he drifted off to sleep, he heard what sounded like a voice from heaven. Suddenly his wife woke him, saying, "Mike, why are you making that moaning noise?"

Astonished, he said, "I heard a voice saying, 'You will call crows,' and I was calling them." They laughed so hard they almost couldn't get back to sleep.

Sometimes the message you think you've received is *not* from God. It may be your imagination working overtime, or it might be an old "tape" from childhood, playing in your head. Sometimes, like those in Mike's dream, the words that pop into your dreams or thoughts are nonsense, but other times, they can be downright dangerous. Especially that sweet little voice that whispers "Want it? Charge it!" So maybe calling crows might be a lot safer than visiting the mall.

For Further Reflection

1. Are you relying on your own good sense and the Scriptures, or do you want a sudden revelation?
2. What message are you hearing in your mind?
3. Do they agree with what God has already shown us?

Prayer

Teach me to know your voice, Lord, and help me to ignore any others. Amen

Reaping the Whirlwind

They sow the wind and reap the whirlwind.
　　　　　　　　　—Hosea 8:7

My downfall is *print*. Things with print on them, like books and magazines. Books are crowding us out of our house! We have bookshelves in every room—and they're all double-stacked. Dresser drawers are full of books, and so are boxes under the beds. None of this is bad; books are fine things, even noble things to own. But what *is* wrong is that I read many of those books only once.

Today I was straightening a bookcase when a top stack of books fell on me and knocked me off my step stool. My husband rushed in to find me on the floor, surrounded by volumes. "Did the books attack?" he joked.

"I'm reaping the whirlwind," I said. I foolishly sowed the wind by spending a lot of money on books I could have obtained from the public library and read once. Now I was reaping what I had sown: I was up to my neck in both books and debt.

"Take these to the secondhand bookstore," I told my husband. "Sell them. Oh, and take these and these and these. . . ."

Whirlwinds *can* be stopped.

⚖ For Further Reflection

1. Did you sow the wind through foolishness, and reap a whirlwind?
2. How is that "whirlwind" manifesting in your life?
3. How will you stop the storm?

⚖ Prayer

Lord Jesus, you spoke to the tempest and it subsided. Bring peace to my life. Amen

A Dinner of Stones

*The tempter came to him and said, "If you are the
Son of God, tell these stones to become bread."*
— Matthew 4:3

I had saved up enough register slips from the su-
permarket to qualify for a premium. I enjoyed looking through the catalog, trying to choose my
hard-earned plunder. Would I prefer a lace table-
cloth, a silver-plated tray, or an electric skillet? I finally settled on dinner for two at a fine local
restaurant, and headed to the market. I strode back
to the customer service counter and looked up at
the sign that read, *Register slip redemption center*.

Redemption center!

Oh, boy. I was about to turn stones into a fancy dinner, collecting my award for what amounted to greed.

Under the sign was another one that read, "You
may convert your slips into cash for a local charity."
I handed over my envelope and named the food-for-
the-homeless charity I'd wanted to benefit.

The clerk smiled. "We will donate fifty dollars to them," she said.

Debts or no debts, I wasn't going to risk God's displeasure by neglecting those who have a lot less than I do. And God's redemption premiums last longer than dinner.

For Further Reflection

Turning stones into bread is always a temptation. But God's grace can help you overcome any temptation. Resolve to put acquisitiveness behind you and embrace a giving attitude.

Prayer

Lord Christ, you resisted the Enemy when he tempted you. Grant me that same strength. Amen

Crossing on Dry Land

> *But the Israelites went through the sea on dry ground, with a wall of water on their right and on their left.*
>
> —Exodus 14:29

One of our creditors was threatening a court action.

I prayed at my bedside, sure all was lost; I saw no solution to our predicament. Like the Israelites, I could only see disaster all around. The company thundered like Egyptians in back of us, demanding payment in full. Damaged credit became a wall on our right, and loss of funds loomed on the left. I thought we would drown in the financial flood as we got further and further behind.

Then I heard God's still small voice, promising to supply all our needs. It didn't happen instantly, but we found a way to meet the creditor's demand without taking food out of our mouths or selling the house. That day I fell to my knees in gratitude.

Crossing through tough financial times isn't pleasant, but it's easier when God is parting the waters. Today I'm going to remember that God will supply everything I need.

For Further Reflection

1. Do you let fear and panic hide God's presence?
2. Are you listening for God's reassurance?

Prayer

Thank you, dear Lord, for parting the waters. Amen

The Hammer

They fasten it with hammer and nails so it will not totter.

—Jeremiah 10:4

I probably have the worst mechanical skills in the nation. I keep a small hammer in my desk to tack up photographs and calendars, and today I couldn't even do that without slamming into my thumb.

No wonder my life is such a mess, I thought as I stood in the bathroom with cold water running over my throbbing thumb. *If I'd had any talent with tools or any manual dexterity, I might have had a great career as an engineer or computer builder. I'd have plenty of money and my debts would be paid.*

But I *do* have the talent and tools I need to get out of debt. I write books that make money. Carpenters don't have to create poetry, and thank heaven, I don't have to make a living nailing things on walls. Every one of us debtors has a talent or a skill that can contribute to society, and also be the answer to financial need.

For Further Reflection

Are you trying to hammer your way into an occupation you're not suited for? Do you fear that if you did make writing or preaching or painting your vocation, you'd fail or make too little money? Journal your answers, and pray about what God is calling you to do.

Prayer

God, when you call me, help me hear what you're calling me to do. Amen

Fresh Air

But it is the spirit in a man, the breath of the Almighty, that gives him understanding.
—Job 32:8

The cabin door stuck fast and I gave it a yank. When the door popped open, a roomful of stale air rushed out—with an odor something like mildew mixed with old gym socks and a hint of kerosene. I was determined to spend a pleasant weekend here in the mountains, so I flung open all the windows. It took hours to air out the place, but after a while the scent of pine took over the bad smell.

Sometimes I prefer not to inspect my finances as often as I should. I'd rather ignore any hint that I might be overspending. If I keep the ledger closed long enough but continue to spend, I am certain to get a malodorous surprise someday soon.

Before my budget begins to reek from neglect, I'm going to open that ledger. I'll stay on top of my finances before they get out of control. Being in charge of my money will be like a breath of fresh air.

For Further Reflection

If you're *still* hiding from the facts about your debts, open the window and let in a breath of fresh air. Sit down and read through your bills.

Prayer

Jesus, I'm scared to look at the facts again. Give me courage. Amen

Return Counter

He is the stone you builders rejected, which has become the capstone.

—Acts 4:11

Some days I feel like a garment tossed on a department store's return counter. Those are the days when the mail is full of rejection slips for what I've written, when my efforts to get out of debt feel futile, and when I can't stand my face in the mirror. I can almost hear the world saying to the clerk, "Inferior quality. Please take her back."

But the clerk turns out to be God, who says, "Wait a minute. I made this woman myself, and nobody can send her back." The world may reject me or—more likely, I reject myself—but God is always there, holding up a lifetime warranty.

How can I get off the return counter and back into life? The usual ways: prayer, Bible study, and action. So for today, my prayer is that I will remember I am worthy of God's love. I'll study all the

Bible passages that show how Christ was rejected. And I'll take the kind of action that reflects new resolve to keep going on my plan.

✍ For Further Reflection

Do you sometimes feel worthless and discarded? Jesus experienced being despised and rejected, and he's sharing your feelings with you.

✍ Prayer

King of my life, thank you for lifting me when I fall and drying my tears. Amen

A Joyful Song

*Sing to the Lord, for he has done glorious things; let
this be known to all the world. Shout aloud and sing
for joy, people of Zion, for great is the Holy One of
Israel among you.*

—Isaiah 12:5, 6

A friend's grandmother had taught music in ele-
mentary schools for forty years. Then "Grams," as
my friend called her, suffered a devastating stroke.
One side of her body was paralyzed, and she was
frustrated that she no longer could speak. But
Grams had a secret weapon—she still could sing.
When Grams sang the children's tune "Jesus Loves
Me," her face lit up with joy.

Money woes can paralyze my life if I let them.
Sometimes I have trouble counting my blessings
when too much debt threatens to overwhelm me.
When finances try to knock me down, I can forget
to be grateful for what's good in my life.

Today I will give thanks. My debts won't disappear, but they don't have to consume me. I can sing a song, just to remind myself of the joys in life.

🕮 For Further Reflection

Whether you're a monotone or ready for opera, your singing is a way to praise God. Today, when possible, sing as you work or drive or clean or care for children.

🕮 Prayer

Teach me joy through song, Great Singer. Amen

Stars in My Bones

... become blameless and pure, children of God
without fault in a crooked and depraved generation,
in which you shine like stars in the universe ...
                                        —Philippians 2:15

One of the hardest things to do is overcome what I've been told I am. For many years I had a sense of unworthiness, as if I were a liability to the universe. I thought I was the brainless, selfish, flighty fool I'd been told I was. Living out someone else's idea of me helped me get into debt: How could I be expected to be wise and capable?

But when God created the stars and galaxies, their hydrocarbon dust drifted throughout the universe; that dust still floats through the universe and settles on Earth. Scientists say the very clay of Earth, the material from which God made the first man, is full of stardust. So along with the breath of God in my lungs, I also have stars in my bones.

God doesn't make mistakes. The tiny particles of

stars in my body mean that I'm important in God's sight. And I no longer have to believe that I'm silly or worthless.

And I can order life around me in the same way this marvelous universe is ordered. A neat office! A clean kitchen! And bills paid on time! I can do it— after all, I'm made out of stars.

For Further Reflection

When you consider your origins, do you limit your understanding to biology? Think about having stars in your bones, and then meditate on how that affects your indebtedness.

Prayer

God of earth and heaven, you have ordered the universe and set it in motion. Thank you for making me part of that plan. Amen

Winter Wind

As long as the earth endures, seedtime and harvest,
cold and heat, summer and winter, day and night will
never cease.

—Genesis 8:22

I spent two years in a Plains state where the wind never stopped. In the spring, the strong breeze made waves in the gold-green wheat fields. The summer gusts could be dangerous, turning into tornadoes and pelting the city with hail. Wind in autumn wiped red and gold leaves off the trees and sent them dancing down the street. And the winter wind went through me like a chain saw cutting logs. No matter how much I bundled up during the winter, I was never really warm, and I felt as if the cold would last forever.

But when spring came, winter's icy wind gave way to lilac-scented breezes and soft evening zephyrs. I forgot blizzards and icicles and snow flying in the gusts while I basked in the sunshine and picked wild violets in the fragrant woods by the river. Winter? Did we have winter?

Being in debt is like a fierce, freezing winter wind that bites through you. But spring is coming with the day when everything is paid in full. And when that happens, you can think, Debt? Was I ever in debt?

⮑ For Further Reflection

Are you living in a perpetual winter, with the icy breath of debt freezing your soul? Make a list of things you'll do to make the spring of a debt-free life a reality.

⮑ Prayer

Deliver me from the frost and cold of indebtedness, and teach me spring. Amen

Black Holes

*Now the earth was formless and empty, darkness was
over the surface of the deep, and the Spirit of God
was hovering over the waters.*

—Genesis 1:2

To astronomers, a black hole is a region of space
with so much mass concentrated in it that there is
no way for a nearby object to escape its gravita-
tional pull. These mysterious areas are places where
stars and other celestial bodies are literally sucked
inside. Even light can't escape. Some scientists think
objects might be able to exit from the other side,
through a "wormhole."

When I'm in debt over my head, I feel as if I've
fallen into a black hole of my own. I didn't escape
the temptation to use credit cards, and I'm hanging
on for dear life to my pride. I've allowed myself to
get sucked in by the lie that tells me I can have it all.

But light is at the bottom of the debt hole. Today, I can let that pride be destroyed. I can admit
that my spending is out of control. I can seek fi-

nancial counseling and learn what it takes to break free. With a little help, I'll come out on the debt-free side of the galaxy.

For Further Reflection

1. Do you ever get sucked into the black hole of debt?
2. Can you find your way out?
3. What help do you need from God?

Prayer

Deliver me from overwhelming forces, O God, and destroy my pride so I can get free. Amen

Crocodiles in the River

A prudent man sees danger and takes refuge, but the simple keep going and suffer for it.

—Proverbs 22:3

I'm your basic animal lover, but I really dislike alligators and crocodiles. They eat everything, they hunt relentlessly, and they have tiny reptilian brains. I can't think of anything worse than falling into a river full of crocodiles. And that's what living with debt is like: swimming in the Nile delta, with slit-eyed crocodiles slithering toward me through the rushes. I'd be lucky if I got out of that river, maimed but alive.

Fortunately, I don't have to stay in the river of debt, watching desperately for alligators or sharks or piranhas or any other dangerous creature. By facing up to my debts and doing something to start getting free of them, I've moved into safer waters, where the fiercest creature is a graceful rainbow trout.

When I look back at my indebtedness, I realize God was in those dangerous waters with me, waiting to hear me yell for help. When I did, God showed me how to swim to safety.

For Further Reflection

1. What kind of river are you swimming in? Are you in dangerous waters?
2. Do you believe God is with you in those waters?
3. How has God helped you out of danger?

Prayer

Lord, I know you are always with me. Help me out of dangerous waters. Amen

The Eden Diet

*And the Lord God commanded the man, "You are
free to eat from any tree in the garden; but you must
not eat from the tree of knowledge of good and evil,
for when you eat of it you will surely die."*

—Genesis 2:16, 17

A woman in my Bible study said, "Well, God shouldn't
have told them not to eat that fruit. He *knew* they
would go right for it, then. That's human nature."

Forbidden fruit dangles from the branch more
attractive than an everyday diet. Most theologians
believe that our tendency to pick that fruit proves
humanity's fallenness.

But the couple in Eden hadn't fallen when God
gave them their food restrictions. They had an opportunity to live forever by eating from the tree of
life, and to nourish their perfect bodies with the
other fruits in the garden. The Eden diet offered
sweetness and life, while eating fruit from the pro-
scribed tree meant expulsion and pain.

Making bad choices has been with us ever since Eden, but we have the power to stop that pattern. I don't have to keep charging things on my credit card just because Eve ate poison fruit. I'm going back to the Eden diet of obedience.

For Further Reflection

1. What forbidden fruit do you keep eating?
2. Are you strong enough to offer God complete obedience?
3. Are you excusing your credit habits as "human nature"?

Prayer

I want to follow you, Lord; I want to be like Jesus. Amen

Waterfall

I heard a voice from heaven like the sound of many waters and like the sound of loud thunder.
—Revelation 14:2

I was ready to turn back. The stony hillside was steep enough to make my ankles ache, and my face was scratched by brambles and saplings.

"Please," my teenaged son said. "Just a little farther and we'll be there." So I pushed onward, as snapping branches slashed my arms and blackberry vines scratched through my jeans.

Soon I heard a rushing, roaring sound like thunder. A moment later we broke through the thicket to see a waterfall with three small cascades leaping over the dark basalt. Firs and vine maples leaned inward to make a canopy that filtered the sun. Thick fairy moss surrounded the stream like velvet upholstery. Calypso orchids and fawn lilies nodded from every crevice, and over the entire scene, a rainbow arched like the angel of the falls. I have never seen a holier place.

What if I had turned back? I never would have seen that glorious sight, would never have shared my son's excitement. The climb had been hard, but I forgot about jagged branches and brambles the moment I beheld the waterfall scene.

I've wanted to turn back several times while I was working my way out of debt. But then I would never experience the moment of being debt-free. The climb is worth what lies at its end.

For Further Reflection

1. Do you feel like turning back in your climb out of debt?
2. What will you see and hear when you reach the top?
3. Do you have someone to encourage you?

Prayer

Give me the strength of purpose to go on, God, to behold your glory. Amen

Prudence

O simple ones, learn prudence; O foolish men,
pay attention.

—Proverbs 8:5

In earlier times, many parents named their daughters "Prudence," perhaps hoping that the girls would grow up to be thrifty and circumspect. One of my favorite storybook characters was called Little Prudy, who did indeed become cautious, discreet, and modest. But I never identified with that little paragon: I thought I was more like Prudy's younger sister Alice, called Dotty Dimple. She was naughty and easily persuaded to do what was forbidden. That image of myself might have been compounded by the fact that my parents' nickname for me was "Dotty," even though they had never read my books, and by the fact that my mother criticized me almost every waking moment.

I think I told myself for years that I was a weak woman without good sense, unable to make deci-

154

sions or manage money. But I'm *not* silly, head-strong Dotty Dimple. The person I thought I had to be wasn't real. The real me is a woman into whom God put prudence and common sense and resolution. I can do all things through Christ, which strengtheneth me.

For Further Reflection

Have you deluded yourself into thinking you're weak and unable to manage? Start today investigating the person God *really* means for you to be.

Prayer

Thank you for the person I am, God, and for the person you are making me into. Amen

Like a Tree

He is like a tree planted by streams of water, which yields its fruit in season and whose leaf does not wither. Whatever he does prospers.

—Psalm 1:3

During the sixties, we loved to sing, "We shall not, we shall not be moved. . . . Just like a tree that grows by the wa-a-ter, we shall not be moved." At that time we used an old hymn to indicate our determination in the fight for school and job integration; but the words ring true forever.

"Shall not be moved" means firm in faith and looking not on debt but on God's plenty. Someone said that when we focus on abundance, life feels abundant, and when we focus on lack, life feels lacking. That isn't a magic incantation I can use to think myself rich; it's remaining unmoved, even in adversity. What I focus on is what I will be aware of, and if I keep my faith and belief that God will help me with any problem, I can stay right here, grow-

ing by the streams of water and bearing fruit in
season.

For Further Reflection

Are you able to remain unmoved in your
faith, hope, and charity even while you struggle? Today, make a list of abundances you can
see in your life.

Prayer

*Keep me by the stream, Lord, and let me bear fruit.
Amen*

Bat Bridge

*Because you are my help, I sing in the shadow of
your wings.*

—Psalm 63:7

People in Austin, Texas, like to gather after sunset
on a bridge over Town Lake. Soon dark, whirring
silhouettes fill the air as flock after flock of bats rise
into the evening. They call it the "Bat Bridge," and
the sight of a million or so bats winging through
the dusk is awe-inspiring and a little bit scary. But
we'd be afflicted with more mosquitoes and stinging gnats and other flying insects if bats didn't gobble them up.

People around the world have differing feelings
about bats. Here in the United States, we perpetu-
ate silly legends that bats nest in women's hair, or
that they drink blood from your neck. But in China,
the free-flying exuberant bat is considered a symbol
of joy, and china for wedding banquets is often em-
bossed with red bat shapes as a wish for happiness.

Getting out of debt is like a sudden flight of bats. I can either cower before the idea in fright, covering my hair with my hands and remembering Dracula stories—or I can embrace the process with joy. It's all a matter of where you stand on the bridge.

For Further Reflection

Are you afraid of bats? What's more important, are you so afraid of finance and numbers that you're scared to get out of debt? Take a deep breath and think of debt repayment as an opportunity for joy.

Prayer

Thank you, Great Creator, for bats and birds and butterflies and all things with wings. Amen

New Vision

And there before me was the glory of the God of Israel, as in the vision I had seen in the plain.

—Ezekiel 8:4

I was overdue for new glasses. When I finally slipped them on, I was amazed at the bright colors around me. I hadn't *really* seen everything in my environment for months, and when I did, the world looked new.

As I gradually change what we owe to what we've paid, I see everything differently. Once the world looked dark and dreary because the burden of indebtedness—and seeing no way out—made me depressed. Now, even when rain pours down, as it often does here in the Northwest, I feel sunny inside and life looks bright. Getting out of debt is like a new vision, a fresh stimulation for living my life.

When you start easing up on money problems, your vision of God changes, too. Instead of a faraway deity who looks down at you with remote sympathy, you start realizing that God is in the struggle with you, deflecting some of the blows and anesthetizing pain. God is the inspiration that makes the fight for financial freedom worth it all.

For Further Reflection

1. What is your vision for the future?
2. Does it include the presence of God?
3. Are you seeing your situation clearly and new each day?

Prayer

Be Thou my vision, O Lord of my life. Amen

My Roll of the Dice

Lord, you have assigned me my portion and my cup;
you have made my lot secure.

—Psalm 16:5

When David wrote the Psalm about his "portion and cup," he wasn't talking about food. He refers to a game of lots in which your *portion* is the pile of tokens you've accumulated; you shake the numbered tokens in the *cup* and pour them out on a table. Instead of depending on luck, David attributed his success to God. He was saying, in essence, "God, you're my roll of the dice; I'll take you for my lot in life."

Until now, you may have been thinking about money in terms of either luck or hard work, depending on windfalls and wages, without acknowledging God as the one source of everything. That's turning life into a gamble instead of looking to the graciousness of God, and buying the world's message! Luck won't get you or me out of debt;

strength of purpose will, and I can get that from God.

✍ For Further Reflection

1. Have you been gambling with your life?
2. Do you depend on God for everything?
3. Write out a prayer, surrendering your future to God.

✍ Prayer

You are my all in all, O Christ, and in you I am safe. Amen

Rejoicing Flowers

The desert and the parched land will be glad; the
wilderness will rejoice and blossom.

—Isaiah 35:1

Flowers are God's laughter. Every floret is full of
humor and rejoicing: Blossoms dance on the breeze
and branches willingly bend under their weight.
The first flowers of spring are unexpected gifts.
Every winter, I forget how spring looks until the
first crocus appears. Soon jonquils and yellow for-
sythia emerge, the drab quince bushes burst into
burgeoning color, and nearly every tree in my
neighborhood becomes a pink cloud.

The day I get all the way out of debt, the day I
actually write the last check for an overdue bill, my
life will feel like spring, with its promise of new life
and fresh beginnings. Maybe we won't see any lilacs
or pink trees, but my step will be light and my smile
will tell the world that I'm into a different season.

In fact, I think that on that day, I'll empty my

change jar—actually a little blue pitcher in my bedroom where I drop my dimes and quarters—and go buy a bouquet for my coffee table. And then I'll sit on the couch in front of God's gift of laughter.

✍'For Further Reflection

Bring some spring into your life, no matter what time of year it is: Pick or buy some flowers, arrange them in a vase, and say a prayer of thanksgiving for God's helping you pay your debts.

✍'Prayer

It's always spring where you are, Lord. Thank you for flowers and for joy. Amen

Tom Thumb Wedding

You are the children of the Lord your God.
—Deuteronomy 14:1

When I was ten I sang a solo in a "Tom Thumb Wedding," starring a pair of three-year-olds. Some preschool boys were ushers. Bridesmaids with rouged cheeks ranged in age from two to five.

Everyone in town flocked into the high school auditorium for this romantic event. When I started singing "O Promise Me," everyone began to laugh. They laughed all through my song and I was close to tears, wondering if I looked funny in my silky blue dress, or if I was singing off-key. Finally I looked over my shoulder to discover that the little groom was flinging flowers through the air, running in circles to catch them, and even chewing them up. I had worked hard, but few people applauded because they couldn't hear me sing.

My debts are like the little bridegroom, distracting attention. My friends probably don't appreciate how hard I'm working to be free; they just see the debts. But one of these days I won't owe anybody, and then I can stand up and let the world hear my life song. Until then, God is the one applauding.

For Further Reflection

1. Are you content to let God alone know your progress?
2. Do you feel annoyed because your family or friends aren't applauding?
3. Are you willing to tell God how you feel, and accept God's blessing?

Prayer

You're the only one who knows everything about me, God. Thanks for loving me anyway. Amen

Facing the Truth

O Lord, do not your eyes look for truth?
—Jeremiah 5:3

Sometimes I rationalize my definition of "I am": I *am* going to lose twenty pounds, but it's been raining for three weeks so I can't go walking. I *am* outgoing, but my work keeps me tied to my office, so I don't have time for socializing. I *do* keep a neat, organized office—the mess I make when I'm working is just a transitory phase.

And I *am* thrifty and money-wise; my indebtedness is a temporary result of—what?

Uh-oh. I can't think of an excuse. I'll have to face the truth that I'm in debt because I haven't been wise about spending, and now I'm literally paying the piper.

Funny. A heavy weight just slid off my shoulders. My mind is calm because it isn't frantically looking for answers. When I finally quit defining "I am" and look the truth straight in the eye, I actually feel relieved. And if I'd done this five years ago, I wouldn't be in debt at all.

ℬ For Further Reflection

1. Are you facing the truth about your indebtedness?
2. Do you rationalize to keep from feeling pain?
3. Can you be honest with yourself from now on?

ℬ Prayer

Because you are always in present time, God, you are. Amen

Window to God

I'm severely allergic to bee and wasp sting, so I stay inside a lot during the late-summer yellow jacket season. When other people are barbecuing or sitting on their front porches or gardening, I depend on windows. They show me the sunshine and let me hear the birds or the wind in the tall fir trees that grow in the woods behind our house. I can see the wild roses blooming on the hillside below the fir trees, and hear the songs of the goldfinches and pine siskins that swoop through the blackberry brambles.

Prayer is my window to God, my opening to divine presence, my way of knowing that God is as real as the birds or the flowers. Just as I gaze out of my windows in the late summer to enjoy the trees and sunshine, so my prayers let me see God with my inner vision. Without prayer, without the God in my life, I'd never be able to pay off my debts, or have the strength to press toward the mark.

For Further Reflection

1. How much time do you spend in prayer?
2. Do you open the window to God's presence, and allow yourself to bask in love?
3. Without prayer, could you keep going?

Prayer

You are as close as my prayers, Lord. Thank you. Amen

Sand Garnets

The sacred gems are scattered at the head of
every street.

—Lamentations 4:1

I discovered the first one near an anthill in the desert: a small garnet, gleaming against the flame-colored Sonoran sand. Fifteen minutes later, I had a handful, and a half hour later, I unearthed a heavy piece of white quartz with a dark red garnet, the size of a fingernail, embedded in its surface.

I keep the garnet quartz on my desk, partly as a paperweight but most of all as a reminder that treasure is always waiting for me to find it. Sometimes the treasure is a word or phrase I need for something I'm writing. Sometimes it's an unexpected word of encouragement or love. And sometimes the treasure I come across is *innovation*: the ability to come up with a creative, money-saving answer to something like a gift or a household need or a travel situation.

God filled me with creativity, and also furnishes enough strength to turn my imagination into something fun and useful.

For Further Reflection

Are you using your imagination to stay out of new debt? List ten birthday or Christmas gifts you could devise without spending more than a dollar on each one.

Prayer

O God, thank you for the treasures you set before us in life. Amen

Helper Talk

Abraham believed God, and it was credited to him as
righteousness, and he was called God's friend.

— James 2:23

We writers don't always have time to talk among
ourselves, but when we do get together, our words
fly. We discuss character, plot, grammar, article
structure, and style. We chatter about process, tri-
umphs, and disappointments. Even writers who
don't know one another well can enter into "shop
talk" with impunity, and our talks make writing
easier.

Getting out of debt became easier when I found
a friend who was also struggling. Like two writers,
we can talk about our progress, our attempts at
debt reduction, and where we are in the payment
process. We've encouraged each other during difficult moments and cheered each other's successes.

Nothing is quite so bad when you share it with a
friend. That's why God made Eve as a helper to

Adam, saying the man should not live alone. When you can find another person who has the same problem you do, you can lift each other up instead of falling down all alone.

For Further Reflection

1. Are you willing to have helpers in your life and work?
2. Are you so embarrassed about your debts that you discourage intimacy with another?
3. Where can you find a friend to share this process?

Prayer

Please, God, send me a friend to share my experience. Amen

Cactus Wrens

*. . . your dwelling place is secure, your nest is set in
a rock.*

—Numbers 24:21

In the early spring on the desert, a swift, elegant
brown bird nests on top of the saguaro cacti. By
April, blossoms whiter than cream appear on those
same cactus tops. The chicks are fledged by the
time the stiff white flowers open, and this used to
be a cause of great wonder and anxiety to me. Over
and over I asked my parents and my first grade
teacher how the wrens, or how the cactus, knew
how many chicks there were. I asked, "But what if
one bird was very little and couldn't fly yet; would
it fall out when the flowers opened? What if it fell
on the rocks or a bobcat ate it?" I worried about this
late at night and during mealtimes, so that by late
spring I could hardly eat or sleep. Finally my father
told me, "God made all creatures so they know
their times, and they are obedient."

God planted this same sense of time inside me. I know that today. I'm getting out of debt, and flying free.

For Further Reflection

1. Do you have a sense of time and season in your life?
2. Are you as obedient to God's will as the wild animals and birds?
3. How does the world try to interfere with God's times?

Prayer

I give thanks to you, God, for signs and seasons and the times you have appointed. Amen

Light in the Trees

*The Lord is my light, and my salvation; whom shall
I fear?*

—Psalm 27:1

We were camping at a state park in the California
redwood forest. One evening we drove into the
nearby beach city to see a movie, and on the way
back late at night, we saw no sign of civilization on
the dark, tree-lined road. Were we lost? Didn't we
make this loop before? Finally one of my daughters
said, "Look! Lights! Lights in the trees!"

Sure enough, someone's Coleman lantern was
gleaming through the redwood branches. We drove
in that direction and saw a family playing cards at
the table beside their campfire. Our campsite was
just a little farther down that road, and the lantern
light had been like a welcome sign. As we piled out
of the car and got ready to sleep in our tent, I kept
glancing with gratitude toward the light that flick-
ered through the trees.

Getting to the end of debt is like that light in the trees, a "welcome home" sign that tells me I'm doing the right thing.

✍ For Further Reflection

1. Can you see light gleaming through your indebtedness?
2. Make a list of helpful "signals" in your life that have helped you learn wisdom about money.

✍ Prayer

Be the light in my darkness, Lord, and lead me home safely. Amen

Sea Monkeys

We must no longer be children, tossed to and fro and blown about by every wind of doctrine, by people's trickery, by their craftiness in deceitful scheming.
—Ephesians 4:14

A few years ago, toy and novelty stores sold "sea monkeys," small creatures that would, according to the exuberant ads, dance and cavort as soon as you put them into water; the box contained a square plastic container like a fishbowl. I know a number of people who bought them, but I know none who saw any movement at all, much less cavorting and fancy swimming. "Sea monkeys" were just tiny dried shrimp that couldn't be revived.

In our family, we use the term to describe products or services that look like scams or are worthless. Offers of "free vacations" and no-cost travel clubs are sea monkeys. A lot of highly advertised garden tools and exercisers qualify.

And so do credit cards that advertise one percent

interest; they soon become very expensive. I know. I've got a wallet full of sea monkeys I need to dispose of.

For Further Reflection

1. Have you ever bought or subscribed to something useless?
2. Does that include too many credit cards?
3. You probably wouldn't buy sea monkeys; but what kinds of scams attract you?

Prayer

O God, you endowed me with the power of discernment. Help me use that power to erase my debts, and avoid new ones. Amen

Bottled Oxygen

How can I, your servant, talk with you, my Lord?
My strength is gone and I can hardly breathe.
                                          —Daniel 10:17

A few climbers have ascended Mt. Everest without bottled oxygen, and they have reason to brag; but their experience doesn't lessen the triumph of those who can't make it to the top without a breathing assist. Most sensible mountain enthusiasts take plenty of oxygen up on that highest peak because at nearly 30,000 feet, the air is thin and unreliable. Certain weather conditions can worsen the situation, so climbers have to be prepared.

Not too many months ago, I felt as if I were smothering. I couldn't breathe under the pile of debt in my life. This time, because I'm up in the rarified atmosphere, the excitement has me almost breathless.

Yes, I'm tired. Yes, at moments, even though the summit is in front of me, I've felt like giving up. Yes, the thin air of financial austerity hasn't given me much breathing room. But the zenith is before me, and now I need some help. Which, of course, means prayer. Prayer is the "bottled oxygen" on the out-of-debt mountain, and as long as I can pray, I can climb.

For Further Reflection

Are you feeling tired and breathless at this point in your climb out of debt? Take a whole day to do nothing but pray, and see how refreshed you are.

Prayer

You are the breath of life, O God, and in you I live and move and have my being. Amen

Jettison

Then they took Jonah and threw him overboard,
and the raging sea grew calm.

—Jonah 1:15

I once led a youth group up the back side of Mr.
Whitney, the highest peak in the contiguous United
States. Jeeps took us up to 10,000 feet; we had to
climb much higher, then descend into a little
canyon where they were to rebuild a Christian
camp lodge that had been destroyed by heavy snow
the year before.

The kids were warned not to bring anything
heavier than a toothbrush or a harmonica, but
many of them ignored our counsel. They brought
cameras, guitars, binoculars, and heavy books; as
the trail led upward, their belongings got too heavy.
One by one, they began to leave things along the
trail, hoping they could retrieve them on the way
back. When we reached 12,000 feet, one boy hung
his guitar and camera by their straps on a juniper

tree; one girl buried her jewelry to protect it from the Sierras' famous pack rats.

In the climb out of debt, I've had to jettison some ideas. I don't really need to have the carpets shampooed regularly. I can live without a new dress for Christmas, and our car is okay for a few more years. Life out of debt is better than all those heavy luxuries.

For Further Reflection

1. What ideas, things, or habits are now too heavy for you to carry?
2. What will you toss away so you can keep climbing?
3. What will be your reward for all this?

Prayer

You lived and died and rose, all without a place to lay your head. Teach me simplicity. Amen

Gratitude

*Let the word of Christ dwell in you richly as you
teach and admonish one another with all wisdom, and
as you sing psalms, hymns and spiritual songs with
gratitude in your hearts to God.*

—Colossians 3:16

In *Attitudes of Gratitude* (Conari Press, 1999), author
M. J. Ryan says, "One of the incredible truths about
gratitude is that it is impossible to feel both the
positive emotions of thankfulness and a negative
emotion such as anger or fear at the same time.
Gratitude births only positive feelings—love, com-
passion, joy, and hope."

Several times while I was fighting the good financial fight, I felt depressed and angry; but as soon
as I fell to my knees in thanksgiving for God's good-
ness and majesty and presence and help, my un-
happiness disappeared. So although I'm not cursed
with bitterness or fear today, I am going to spend
the next twelve hours in gratitude.

Thank you, God. Thank you for showing me what to do. Thank you for giving me strength and courage to make hard decisions. Thank you for helping me up the mountain. And thank you for a loving friend and a cooperative husband.

Thanks most of all for insight, God, without which I could not have understood the process I was going through. Amen

For Further Reflection

Keep a gratitude diary. At the end of every day, write down at least one thing you are grateful for, and then say a prayer of thanksgiving.

Prayer

Thank you, Lord. Amen

Stumbling

*Like the blind we grope along the wall, feeling our
way like men without eyes. At midday we stumble as
if it were twilight.*

—Isaiah 59:10

I can't tell you how many times I have stumbled this
past year. Once I started to cry when I realized I
couldn't renew my favorite magazine subscription.
Another time, I was so depressed about money I
bought some expensive chocolate truffles and ate
them all. And when I thought I'd finished a debt but
discovered I had two more payments, I got so upset
that I had to walk up in the hills until I recovered
my composure.

But stumbling isn't the same as crashing. I *did*
cancel the magazine and learned to live without it.
I repented of the chocolate truffles—which went
straight to my thighs—and repaid the money to our
account by skipping the lunch our writers' critique
group attends. And while I was in the hills, sulking,

I glimpsed a doe with a fawn, and realized how beautiful God's world is.

A stumble is just a momentary lapse, not a reason to throw in the towel.

For Further Reflection

1. When you stumble, do you feel ready to give up?
2. Do you remember to keep going on faith, not feelings?
3. How will you feel when your austerity program is over and you're out of debt?

Prayer

Catch me when I stumble, Lord, and remind me that you always will. Amen

Setting Up Goals

After beginning with the Spirit, are you now trying to attain your goal by human effort?

—Galatians 3:3

During a political campaign, we hear daily results of polls. "Polls" may rhyme with "goals," but they're certainly different. Pollsters question many people, and list all their opinions, but to work toward a goal—like getting out of debt—I need to have one focus.

Paying my bills isn't like politics. I can't poll everyone I know and ask them for advice about money, then try to please the most voters. Instead, I have to keep my eyes on the end, on getting my bills paid and *staying* on a cash basis.

I'm not doing it alone, and if I think I am, I'm in trouble. God is both the question and the answer; only God knows what I should do and when I should do it. And I feel certain that on the day when I'm completely out of debt and tempted to congratulate myself, I'll look back and realize that God was doing it the whole time.

And what will I do with my time when that day comes? I'd better ask God.

For Further Reflection

Your goal for a long time has been to get out of debt. Begin, now, to let God help you create some new goals to use after that dream is fulfilled.

Prayer

I press forward to the mark, God. Don't let me slip and fall now. Amen

Help on the Trail

The Lord is with me; he is my helper. I will look in triumph on my enemies.

—Psalm 118:7

In his book *Pilgrim's Regress*, C. S. Lewis writes about the young man John, who is trying both to escape the "Landlord"—God—and to get through a mountain pass. His companion has disappeared, he's out of food, and he feels close to fainting or falling. Finally, he begins to shout, "Help! Help!"

A Man appears to help him up the rocky divide, and John feels horror when he takes the proffered hand. "I've been *praying*," he says. "Praying! It's the Landlord all over again!"

Sometimes I want God's presence, but at other times I prefer to do it all myself. And when I'm in a real bind, I find myself praying when I didn't intend to. And though I'd love to say, "I was deep in debt and got out all by myself," that wouldn't be true. I could never have made it without the Man whose compelling love from the cross gave me the strength and purpose to go on.

For Further Reflection

1. How do you pray for help?
2. Do you treat God as an intruder?
3. How far would you have gotten in debt repayment without God?

Prayer

You are my help in every need. You do my every hunger feed. Amen

A Willing Heart

*Jesus reached out his hand and touched the man.
"I am willing." he said.*

—Luke 5:13

One of my piano teachers, a man with wild gray hair and a slightly manic disposition, often proclaimed with a heavy German accent, "A pianist has the good willing."

"The good willing" meant a heart open to learning, a heart so aligned with the music that the student could play a piece exactly as the composer wrote it. Stubbornness, a closed mind, the refusal to learn, saying a piece was too hard—these, to that teacher, suggested moral turpitude. If any of his students lacked the good willing, he sent them home with the instructions not to come back. During my first lesson with him, my fingers trembled so that I could hardly play the difficult music I was studying.

But to my surprise, he sat down on the bench

beside me, put his hand on my shoulder, and said, "You're trying hard. I know you have the good willing. Now, try to relax and really play the music."

When it comes to getting out of debt, I've had a willing heart. Now all I have to do is relax and play the music: the song that goes, "I can see clearly now. . . ."

For Further Reflection

1. Do you bring a willing heart to your debt problem?
2. Are you hiding any stubbornness or self-pity from yourself?
3. How can you make yourself more open to God's direction?

Prayer

Jesus, you were willing to go to the cross for me. Give me a willing heart also. Amen

The Animal Farm

The hardworking farmer should be the first to
receive a share of the crops.
                                        —2 Timothy 2:6

In George Orwell's famous novel, *Animal Farm*, farm beasts overthrow their cruel master, take over the place, and set up a democratic government where the rules state that every creature is equal to every other. But before too long, the pigs take over and become dictators; they march around on two legs, drink alcohol, wear clothes, and have dealings with humans. Eventually they change the rules to read, "Some animals are more equal than others." Eventually nobody can tell the difference between the pigs and greedy humans.

The pigs on my "farm" have been debts. At first, credit is friendly and helpful, but eventually, debt becomes tyranny, marching around a person's life with impunity, and destroying any chance for a happy outcome. In the novel, the animals can never clearly remember the past because the pigs constantly alter history. That's a lot like making excuses or pretending to be happy with a knot in my stomach.

I'm grateful that all tyrants can eventually be overthrown.

✏ For Further Reflection

Debt is a tyrant. Take up arms against it: prayer, determination, and honesty. Tell the "pigs" of indebtedness that *you* are taking over.

✏ Prayer

You came to earth to deliver us from the Prince of this world's tyranny. Deliver me also from tyrants of my own making and choosing. Amen

Sleeping and Waking

I lie down and sleep; I wake again, because the Lord sustains me.

—Psalm 3:5

I feel as if I've been asleep for a year. Maybe twenty years. Now that I'm getting out of debt, I look back at the past and see a dream. I see a woman struggling to fight imaginary giants, wandering as if she'd lost her way, trying to scream for help but unable to make a sound. Being in financial denial and trying to avoid the anguish I felt over debt had made those years dim, sepia-toned, and unreal.

My waking up was slow and gradual. Little by little, I became aware of how to face my problems and how to get a handle on the solutions. That process was easier than I expected, and now I can breathe freely.

Coming back to consciousness has been an adventure. I'm surrounded by light and energy, as if I had walked into a party in my honor. The sun is shining, lighting my path as I leap forward into real life. Good-bye, darkness.

For Further Reflection

1. Have you been partly asleep, dreaming your life instead of living it?
2. Does the real world look scary to you, or are you glad to be here?
3. How can you make sure you stay awake?
4. What do you want to say to God about today?

Prayer

Now that I am awake and alive, Lord, give me a more grateful heart. Amen

Obstacle Course

For I am convinced that neither death nor life,
neither angels nor demons, neither the present nor
the future, nor any powers, neither height nor
depth, nor anything else in all creation, will be
able to separate us from the love of God that is in
Christ Jesus our Lord,

—Romans 8:38

I can hardly believe the words on the invoice: *paid in full*. I feel as if I've run on an army training track with scores of obstacles to clamber over or crawl under or scale. Now I'm running free, toward a life without debt.

I couldn't have done this without God's help. God used my friends to encourage me, and helped me resist the temptation to give up. God granted me strength and courage to keep trying, even when the climb was hard.

Now, how will I live my new life? Will I inch up on debt again, just charging here and there, telling myself I'll pay the bills when I get home, and soon being back where I started?

No. Prayer and my own determination climbed this mountain with me, and with the help of God, I can stay up here in the high country. I'll never get down in the swamplands again.

For Further Reflection

1. Have you gone past your main obstacles in staying out of debt?
2. What are the major skills you've learned?
3. What code words or signals can you send yourself when you're tempted?

Prayer

Amen, Amen, Lord Christ. So let it be, now and forever. Amen

A Land to Possess

See, the Lord your God has given the land to you; go up, take possession . . . do not fear or be dismayed.
—Deuteronomy 1:21

A friend of mine asked today why I keep making myself fail when I try to get out of debt. After she left, I started examining my emotional state, and found a little glimmer of fear. Is it possible that I'm afraid of living debt-free?

Maybe. If I get out from under the weight of money problems, I won't be the same person. I'll have to face the world without the shield of credit cards and bank loans, and I'm not sure I feel good enough about myself to do that.

The Israelites were afraid to cross into the Promised Land, and they gave all kinds of excuses: We're not ready, we're scared of giants, we don't know the lay of the country. Because they wouldn't enter the Promised Land on time, God let them wander in the wilderness for forty years.

Is that what I want for myself? A lifetime of wandering in the desert of debt, instead of having a productive life?

God has shown me a place where I can live free and strong, where the mail will be full of letters and greeting cards instead of bills, and where a telephone ring will mean a friend is calling. When I get there, I'll be ready—and thankful.

For Further Reflection

1. Are you ever afraid of a debt-free future?
2. Does that fear have its roots in low self-esteem?
3. Can you live without credit?

Prayer

Lead me, Lord. Take my hand and help me see the beauty of living your way. Amen

Ninja

But the one who endures to the end will be saved.
—Matthew 10:22

Ninjas were fierce Japanese professional soldiers; in the fourteenth century they trained in the martial arts and hired out for covert operations. But the roots of their name reveals their original quality: In Japanese, *nin* means "to endure" and *ja* is "person." A Ninja was originally someone who endured.

One of the great Ninja masters said, "Ninjutsu (Ninja martial arts) is not something which should be used for personal desires. It is something which should be used when no other choice is available, for the sake of one's country, for the sake of one's lord, or to escape personal danger."

Personal danger! That's what debt is. I want to become a debt Ninja: a person who stays the course, a fierce warrior who endures against the enemy of indebtedness. But just as those soldiers had to train before they could go to battle, I have to learn the hard discipline of living within my means. I'm going to endure.

✍ For Further Reflection

1. Write down three areas of spending that put you in "personal danger" where once you start, it's hard to stop.
2. Plan out *now*, on paper, how you will defeat that danger.
3. Ask God to help you see when you are falling into old habits of indebtedness.

✍ Prayer

Dear God, I can't endure without you. Help me learn discipline. Amen

Gift Competition

Many seek the favor of the generous, and everyone is a friend to a giver of gifts.

—Proverbs 19:6

At the baby shower, I hoped that my present said, "You are worthy, so therefore I am giving you this expensive gift."

But in a secret corner of my heart, I also hoped I'd "won" the gift contest. Mine was the most original and costliest gift there, the one everyone raved about. I had shopped for three days, going to specialty shops and luxury stores, and I charged the gift on my credit card. And as I drove home from the shower that night, I wondered if my motives were really so pure.

After I spent time in prayer, God showed me the truth. Yes, I loved my friend and wanted to give her something nice, but I was competing with the other women at the shower, and though I had the best gift, mine was the most unworthy because it was dishonest. I could have paid cash for a twenty-dollar present, or I could have shared the cost of a bigger item with a couple of the other women. Let's face it: I was showing off.

✍'For Further Reflection

1. When you buy gifts, do you do so in a competitive spirit?
2. Do you hope to make a good impression with your gift giving?
3. What can you do to change this pattern?

✍'Prayer

Lord God, help me give from the heart instead of trying to win. Amen

Way of Life

Be on your guard against all kinds of greed; for one's life does not consist in the abundance of possessions.
—Luke 12:15

Annie Dillard, the Pulitzer-winning writer, said, "The life of sensation is the life of greed; it requires more and more. The life of the spirit requires less and less; time is ample and its passage sweet."

The "life of sensation" she's describing is one where the outer senses—taste, touch, smell, sight and hearing—have to be satisfied all the time. Do I want to smell something nice? I won't bother with fresh air or new-mown grass; instead, I'll buy some aromatherapy candles. If peanut butter or bologna don't satisfy my palate, I'll go out for a gourmet dinner. I can stimulate my hearing with new CDs instead of playing my old favorites. I want some marble chessmen to replace my wooden ones because I like the smooth, heavy surface. And so on.

Dillard is right: that life requires more and more

and more. But the life of the spirit—prayer, reading, friends, taking pleasure in creation and creating—is what can really make me feel satisfied and alive. The "prince of this world" would like me to crave material things, but God is offering me real life.

For Further Reflection

In your journal, try to fill a whole page with the gifts God has given you that cost nothing but that make your life meaningful and rich.

Prayer

Deliver me, O God, from a life of greed, and show me life in the spirit. Amen

Why Do I . . .

He said to his disciples, "Why are you so afraid?
Do you still have no faith?"

—Mark 4:40

I can't find a single place in the Bible where someone asks, "Why am I doing this?" Maybe people
weren't introspective in those days. Or perhaps
daily life was so hard that people didn't often examine their own motives.

But when a terrible storm with giant waves
threatened to capsize the disciples' boat, Jesus asked
them, "Why are you so afraid?" And then he added,
"Have you no faith?"

Are fear and lack of faith the reasons for all ad-
dictive behavior? Perhaps people overeat, take
drugs, drink to excess, or shop-lift because they're
scared of poverty or solitude or other people.
What's more important right now is: do I spend
money I don't have because I'm scared, and because
I don't have faith that God will help me?

Time to take inventory. Not of my debts, but of my fears and my faith. If I'm scared of anything, from spiders to social situations, I need to deal with my fears without going into debt. And if my faith is thin, then I need to feed it with prayer and study and Christian community. Otherwise, my boat might sink in the storm.

For Further Reflection

Fold a piece of paper lengthwise. On the left side, write everything you're afraid of, be it snakes or poverty. On the right side, make a list of all the ways God has intervened in your life to make it better. Keep the list, and add to it every time a little miracle happens to you.

Prayer

Take away my fears, Lord, and give me the good sense to have faith in you. Amen

Keeping the Commandments

You shall not steal; you shall not deal falsely; and you shall not lie to one another.

—Leviticus 19:11

I'd be shocked if someone accused me of stealing or cheating or lying. I've never even shoplifted a roll of candy mints, I don't cheat anyone, and I have a reputation for being open and honest. I never lie.

At least to other people.

But I stole from myself when I ran up debts, and now have to live too frugally to pay them off. I dealt falsely with myself when I tossed a bill away unopened, or told myself it was okay to squeeze one more thing onto my already-loaded credit card. And worst of all, when I pretended I was perfectly happy living in debt, I was telling myself a lie.

All my life, I've heard that God gave us the commandments as a blessing, and now I see the truth of that statement. "Thou shalt not steal" isn't just an admonition against burglary, but also provides a way for me to live in peace with myself.

For Further Reflection

1. What "sins" do you commit against your own life?
2. Can you understand how cheating yourself breaks a commandment?
3. What will you do to become more honest with yourself?

Prayer

O God, thank you for your commandments. Help me to understand how to apply them to my inner life. Amen

A Sea Full of Sharks

*The Lord ... heals the brokenhearted, and binds up
their wounds.*

—Psalm 147:2, 3

Recently a child was attacked by a shark in Florida
and might have died if several people hadn't come
to his aid. While someone dragged the unconscious
lad to safety and kept him from bleeding to death,
his brave uncle wrestled the shark to shore, risking
his own life, and extracted the boy's arm so doctors
could reattach it.

I think the world is like a sea full of sharks. The
difference between the young victim and us is that
he screamed and we hide our injuries. Debt made
me feel as if I were bleeding to death, but I pretended I was fine.

Yesterday I was talking with friends. By listening
between the lines, I realized that Marcy is miserable
about the custody battle with her former husband,
Dana's bad-tempered, aging father has come to live

with her and drives her crazy, and Maria is in terror that her breast cancer will return. All those women are hiding behind smiles and cheerful talk, just as I am.

Next time we meet for lunch, I'm going to confess my indebtedness. Who knows? Someone there may be able to apply a tourniquet.

◌ For Further Reflection

Almost everyone is walking around with some kind of emotional or spiritual wound. Decide that you're going to share the way that being in debt has injured you, and encourage others to talk about what's hurting them.

◌ Prayer

Give me the strength, God, to scream for help when I need it. Amen

Forfeits

I will redeem you with an outstretched arm
and with mighty acts of judgment.

                          —*Exodus 6:6*

When I was a child, we played "forfeits." Each person would hand in a barrette, a shoe, a wallet, or some other belonging, and someone would hold the forfeits, one at a time, over the person's head, saying "Heavy, heavy, heavy hangs over thy head. What must the owner do to redeem it?" "It" would then name a task: The owners would have to play a piece on the piano, sing an obscure song, touch their toes ten times, or perform some outlandish stunt to recover their belonging. Eventually, "It" would name his or her own stunt to redeem an object, and we all hoped it would be something we could laugh at, something hard and humiliating.

I have felt like I was "It" in that game, with debt hanging over my head, naming my own punishment. Until I turned to prayer. As soon as I began pleading with God for help, I was no longer having to perform "stunts" to get out of the debt game. God redeemed me by showing me to the solution and never, ever humiliating me.

✍ For Further Reflection

1. Do you feel as if debt is hanging over your head?
2. What kinds of humiliations have you gone through?
3. How does prayer redeem your life?

✍ Prayer

Thank you, God, for being my help and my redeemer. Amen

Leg Trap

Does a snare spring up from the ground, when it has taken nothing?

—Amos 3:5

A man on my block hates almost everything. He won't have a tree that drops its leaves, and he poured cement in his yard to avoid mowing and weeding. He swears he can hear raccoons and rabbits and little foxes in his yard at night and that they "give him the creeps." His neighbors, including me, wouldn't sign his petition to have the county exterminator kill everything, so he put a cruel leg trap out in the area behind our homes. Such a clamp can torture a beast for hours or days before it finally dies, and the more it struggles, the tighter the trap becomes. Some animals, like foxes, even chew off their paw.

Debt was just such a trap for me. For a long time, I struggled to get free, paying a debt by taking on another one, juggling balances between credit

218

cards, getting consolidation loans but ending up in debt again. The harder I tried, the worse my pain got. I finally saw that the only way to get out of my trap was to spring it, to give up credit altogether. I've started paying everything off. Uncomfortable, but it beats chewing off a paw.

Meanwhile, I wonder if the man on our block has figured out how sticks of wood keep setting off his trap.

For Further Reflection

1. When you feel trapped by debt, what do you do?
2. How can you spring that trap?
3. What part does God play in your getting loose?

Prayer

God, I'm glad that you set no cruel traps. Amen

Mitzvah

And whatever you do, in word or deed, do everything in the name of the Lord Jesus, giving thanks to God the Father through him.

—Colossians 3:17

I was shooting pictures of Native American dancers at a powwow, pictures to go with an article I had written for a travel magazine. A young man garbed in leather and shiny black feathers went into the circle alone and began moving to the rhythm of the drums, and I focused my camera on him. Just then, one of the event's directors asked me to please not take that picture.

"This one is sacred," he explained. "It's the dancer's prayer."

On another occasion, I was interviewing a rabbi about his spiritual life, and he said most of his prayers were his action, the *mitzvah* or good deed he performed.

Prayer doesn't always mean bowing your head

and folding your hands. Taking food to a homeless shelter or visiting someone in prison or even giving good clothing to charity can be forms of prayer. And I think God honors as prayer the efforts people make to get out of debt. Staying away from the mall will be my *mitzvah* for today, because God's world should be free of financial encumbrance.

For Further Reflection

1. In what ways do you do your prayers?
2. Had you ever considered getting out of debt a form of prayer?
3. Do you feel honor-bound to do at least one *mitzvah* every day?

Prayer

Show me how to pray in word and deed, Lord. Make my life a prayer. Amen

Fireflies

*... every perfect gift, is from above, coming down
from the Father of lights, with whom there is no
variation or shadow due to change.*

—James 1:17

On my first warm evening in the midwestern city, I
was transfixed as the lawns and bushes began to
twinkle like Christmas trees. Everywhere I looked,
tiny white lights gleamed, disappeared, and glim-
mered again.

I had never before seen fireflies; we don't have
them in the West, and I wondered why they stayed
east of the Rockies. Other species have hitchhiked
across the country: Gypsy moths and violin spiders,
for instance, climb onto cars and campers and now
have taken up residence in Oregon. And Mediter-
ranean fruit flies now thrive in California. Why
couldn't I start a firefly colony in the Pacific Northwest?

Because gypsy moths wreak havoc in Oregon's

hazelnut orchards, violin spiders have developed a newer, more poisonous strain in the West, and fruit flies from Italy can decimate California's citrus crop. When you transfer a species from its native land, trouble ensues. Beautiful, harmless midwestern fireflies might do serious damage to our forests and crops.

And when I kept transferring balances from one credit card to another, I got deeper in debt and incurred more and more interest! I had to learn a lesson from fireflies.

✍ For Further Reflection

1. What lessons have you learned from nature about life?
2. Have you transferred balances from one credit card to another?
3. Did that hurt you or help you?

✍ Prayer

God of all Creation, you made the world in perfect balance. Human foolishness threatens that environment, just as it threatens financial peace. Teach us, Lord. Amen

Up, Up and Away . . .

Fear and trembling come upon me, and horror overwhelms me. And I say, "O that I had wings like a dove! I would fly away and be at rest. . . ."
— Psalm 55:5, 6

Sometimes I imagine flying away from my troubles. I'd just spread my wings or get into my colorful hot-air balloon, and sail away, leaving debts behind me. I'd look down on the earth and think how pretty it looked from a distance, and I'd land only to eat or rest.

Humans have always dreamed of flying. That's why we like to hang-glide and parasail and get on airplanes. But the sensation of freedom when we're airborne can't substitute for the satisfaction of accomplishment.

So as much fun as having wings might be, I wouldn't really want to abandon my life here. Sure, I sometimes feel burdened and I fantasize about escaping—but deep down, I want the satisfaction of climbing out of the debt pit. Looking back at a job well done beats looking down at earth's blue, green, and brown. And looking at the words "paid in full" on an invoice will even beat owning a hot-air balloon.

For Further Reflection

1. How often do you feel the urge to run away from problems?
2. Do you ever put things off as a way of escaping?
3. How will you feel when you're out of debt?

Prayer

Someday, Lord, I'll fly straight to you. Until then, keep my sense of moral obligation alive. Amen

Transformation

> ... I will tell you a mystery! ... we will all be
> changed, in a moment, in the twinkling of an eye.
> —1 Corinthians 15:51, 52

I took my friend Natalia's five-year-old daughter to the ballet. Not only had she never seen "Swan Lake," but she had never seen her mother—the prima ballerina—on stage before. When Natalia appeared in her white tutu and feathery headdress, the little girl stared and gasped. Finally she turned to me and said, "Will she still be my mother?"

The people in nearby seats chuckled, but the child was serious. She'd seen her everyday mother become someone she didn't recognize, someone from an alien world. After the ballet, when we went backstage, the girl was shy and tongue-tied, even when her mother hugged and kissed her. Eventually, she got used to seeing her mother transformed into a swan or the snow queen or an ascending lark, but that first amazing glimpse stayed in her memory forever.

I wonder if I look different, too. As I work my way out of debt, will my friends and family see the change within me? Once I was careless and a spendthrift; now, I'm a woman who's determined to transform her life. At least I know God can see the difference.

For Further Reflection

Have you changed since you started this book? Start a journal record of your own transformation, writing down changes in your behavior or attitude. Once a week, check your transformation and journal it.

Prayer

You've known me, Lord, since before I was born. Show me how you are transforming my life. Amen

Crossroads

> *Stand at the crossroads, and look, and ask for the*
> *ancient paths, where the good way lies; and walk in*
> *it, and find rest for your souls.*
>
> —Jeremiah 6:16

I had an hour to get to the luncheon. I was making good time, following the directions the hostess had sent me, when I came to a "Y" in the road. I stopped and reread my directions but found no mention of a crossroads. My choice wasn't informed; I had no way of knowing which was the right way. I finally chose the road to the right, and had to turn around after ten miles. I was more than thirty minutes late getting to my destination.

In the same way, I didn't know what I was doing when I started getting into debt. To make things worse, I was in financial denial. So when it came to making good choices, I consistently chose the wrong road. But now when I'm at a crossroads in my financial life, my choice is informed. Now I *know* what happens when I overspend, overcharge, and let the interest build up. I've been over the path before, and I know which way to turn. I won't be late to my own celebration.

For Further Reflection

Are your financial choices informed? Do you understand interest rates and minimum payments? If not, visit a financial counselor at your bank or credit union, and get explanations.

Prayer

I know you're taking the journey with me, Lord; help me to choose the right roads. Amen

Dis-Stress

Relieve the troubles of my heart, and bring me out of my distress.

—Psalm 25:17

Shopping has always been my "de-stressor." No matter how frazzled I felt about my job or my home life, I could find recovery at the mall. A couple of new novels with bright covers, a pair of slacks or a great top, a pair of dangly earrings, and then maybe a frozen yogurt cone to eat on the way home, and I was calm and happy.

Until the credit card bills came. Then my stress level soared again—and I shopped again. Eventually, something had to give, and I knew that meant I had to either lower my anxiety level or abstain from shopping. Or both.

When I got serious about debt reduction, I had to find new ways to deal with stress. I started going to the library for those new novels; while I was there, I volunteered to tell stories to kids in homeless shelters. Instead of buying clothes, I began wearing all those garments I'd pushed into the back of my closet—and some of them were very attractive. When life became too hard, I climbed into a bathtub full of hot water, while soft music played and an inexpensive scented candle burned. And if all those new "de-stressors" failed, I tried prayer, which turned out to be better than ten trips to the mall.

For Further Reflection

Make a list of ten new ways you can reduce your stress without spending money: singing praise songs, deep breathing, swimming, volunteer work, or bead stringing.

Prayer

You are the source of all calm, God. Remind me to turn to you in my distress. Amen

Driving through Fog

The people who walked in darkness have seen a great light; those who lived in a land of deep darkness—on them light has shined.

—Isaiah 9:2

I couldn't even see anything on the road that night. As I traveled back toward my house in the hills, the fog thickened until I had no idea where I was, and streetlights didn't penetrate the mist.

I rolled down the window and stuck my head out, trying to see the center line a foot or two ahead of my car. I kept my speed at about five miles an hour, which meant that a fast daytime trip became a long, frightening journey.

Deep in the thick darkness, I could hear cars on side streets, bumping into each other, with brakes screeching and glass breaking. I almost missed the final turn into my own street, and when I pulled into my driveway, I sobbed with relief. My hair was dripping wet, my heart was pounding, and my own porch light had never looked so good.

I think indebtedness is like that journey. You have to keep trying to see the road ahead and praying for God to show you the "porch light" of financial freedom.

For Further Reflection

1. What causes the most "fog" in your financial situation?
2. How will you get through to the light?
3. How long is the road ahead?

Prayer

Sometimes I feel lost in thick darkness, Lord. Please, guide me to safety. Amen

On Eagles' Wings

As an eagle stirs up its nest, and hovers over its young; as it spreads its wings, takes them up, and bears them aloft on its pinions, the Lord alone guided him . . .

—Deuteronomy 32:11, 12

When eagle chicks are ready to fledge, their parents begin to tear up the nest. They yank part of it away until the little ones are about down to bare rock, usually on a dangerous cliff. Then they give a chick a push off the precipice. As the eaglet starts to fall, he tries to fly—and all at once he's riding home on the pinions, or strong wing feathers, of his parent. Over and over, the eagles repeat this ritual until the young eagles have started to fly. Then the parents rip out the last bit of the nest, and they all begin a new life.

The Bible makes several references to eagles' wings and God's bearing us up on them. God let me stay in my comfortable nest until the day I was ready to fledge, and suddenly my nest began to disintegrate. Over and over I tried to fly, fell, rose home on God's wings, and tried again. I couldn't give up because God kept pushing me.

I'm not accomplished at soaring yet, but my wings are getting stronger and I can look forward to the next phase. God truly bears me up and saves me from disaster.

For Further Reflection

1. Is God pushing you out of a comfortable nest?
2. Do you truly believe that God will catch you as you fall?
3. Ask yourself if you're ready to fly, staying out of new debt.

Prayer

I think I'm ready, God. Don't let me fall. Amen

When Down Is Up

*God made the two great lights—the greater light
to rule the day and the lesser light to rule the
night—and the stars.*

—Genesis 1:16

When I was a child, I dreamed of going to outer
space and looking down at my world. And then in
the warm summer of 1969, men landed on the
Moon, and saw Earth hovering above the moon's
horizon like a blue marble. If you're standing on
the Moon, you have to look *up* at the world. Why
then, at this very moment, I may be hanging upside
down on my planet, looking *down* at the stars!

The title of the sixties' book about college life, *Been
Down So Long It Looks Like Up to Me*, actually spoke
truth about the shape of our universe. So maybe
when I contemplate the "up" world of material belongings, I'm actually gazing into a pit. And though a
life of frugality and bill-paying might look as if it's beneath the one I'm living, I could be staring at heaven!

Astronauts saw our planet in perspective. I need to look at my life on that Earth through God's perspective, and decide what's really important.

For Further Reflection

1. Do you think you're looking up or down at your financial situation?
2. What would help you change your perspective?

Prayer

Lord God, you are King of the Universe. Help me to see as you do. Amen

The Work of Their Hands

. . . repay them according to the work of their hands;
render them their due reward.

—Psalm 28:4

When you borrow money from a friend or relative, you're aware of the person behind the loan. But when you owe money to a department store or a bank or online bookstore, it's easy to forget that anyone is connected to the debt.

Take that online bookstore, for example: *People* created the website. *People* wrote the books; other *people* designed and marketed and published them. *People* at the bookstore's warehouse found the items I ordered and put them in the mail. Still other *people* do the accounting and notify the credit card company. And who sent out those bills? Goats?

The high rate of personal debt in this country may be because it's not. Personal, that is. Like most people, I rarely think about the flesh-and-blood individuals whose livelihood may depend on repayment. That makes this a *people* issue. One I can no longer ignore.

For Further Reflection

1. How often do you think about the human beings connected to your indebtedness?
2. Would you ignore a person talking to you the same way you ignore a bill?
3. What can you do to be aware of human connections to your debt?

Prayer

God, you created each of us in your image. Help me to remember that as I try to get out of debt. Amen

Lightbulb

*And God said, "Let there be light," and there
was light.*

—Genesis 1:3

Cartoonists like to put a lightbulb over a character's
head to show that he or she has a sudden bright
idea. Light! Eureka! I've got it!

Today I should have one of those things over my
own head. I was doing something ordinary when
suddenly I realized that by concentrating so much
on my *debts*, I had ignored the amount I've already
paid off and that I'd found a way to reduce the interest rate on several balances.

Why am I so negative about myself? If a friend
of mine had come this far, I'd be applauding.
Maybe I need a really *big* lightbulb to illuminate my
own life. Today, I'm going to concentrate on the
progress I've made, instead of thinking "In debt . . .
in debt . . . in debt. . . ."

It may be daytime, but I'm going to turn on the

lights and look at what *is*, instead of what hasn't yet
materialized.

For Further Reflection

How far have you come in your effort to get
out of debt? On a sheet of paper or a journal
page, write down every debt you've paid off,
and every one where you're reducing the balance. You've made progress! Find a way to
celebrate today.

Prayer

*God, send your shining light down on me so that
I can see the truth. Amen*

Notes

Notes

Notes

Notes

Notes

Notes

Kristen Johnson Ingram was born in Phoenix, Arizona, went to high school in Los Angeles, and attended college at Arizona State University.

Ingram has written nearly twenty books, numerous issues of *Forward Day by Day*, and about 1500 magazine and newspaper articles. She teaches at writers' conferences, directed Oregon Christian Writers' Conference for four years, and is a photographer. She leads workshops on suicide prevention and directs retreats.

Ingram lives with her husband Ron, a Shi-Tzu named Tai Pan, and Grendel, a criminal cat, in a house at the edge of the woods near the McKenzie River in Springfield, Oregon. There she birdwatches, photographs wildflowers with a macro lens, and looks for the cougar that has been seen in the surrounding hills.